Standard History of Music

A FIRST HISTORY FOR STUDENTS AT ALL AGES

Forty Illustrated Story Lessons in the
Development of Musical Art, Adapted
for Beginners, Musical Clubs, Private
Teaching, Classwork and General Read-
ing, Including an Appendix upon Club
Organization and Management, Together
With a Map of Musical Europe

By

JAMES FRANCIS COOKE

PUBLISHED BY

THEODORE PRESSER COMPANY

1712 Chestnut Street, Philadelphia

A TALK WITH THE READER

This history is intended for four purposes:

(a) To provide a suitable text-book for beginners in the study of musical history in schools, academies, etc.

(b) To provide a text-book on musical history which may be employed by the private teacher of music with individual pupils or with small classes. The book demands no previous experience in the subject of musical history upon the part of the teacher.

(c) To provide music lovers of all ages with the story of musical history told authentically, clearly, entertainingly, and in a logical manner, so that anyone with the desire to get the essential outlines may do so with comparatively little effort.

(d) To provide the material needed for musical clubs studying the subject of musical history for the first time.

The book is divided into forty story lessons. One chapter a week may be studied without adding more than a very slight amount of time to the student's work.

The ten test questions found at the end of each chapter are of especial importance. Whether the student is studying the book in class or privately, these questions should be correctly answered. After completing the work, the teacher will find it advantageous to make an examination by selecting one question at random from each group of ten.

In the cases of very young pupils, the teacher may readily make a suitable division of the work, so that the lessons shall include only those great masters to whom the most space and attention is given.

Readers will find that the book is self-explanatory throughout— no technical term being introduced without an understandable definition, and no foreign word being employed without a phonetic spelling.

The study of musical history should be the most inviting, entertaining, and profitable of all auxiliary musical studies. By reading more advanced histories the teacher may expand the scope of this book and make the class-work even more fascinating. Baltzell's Musical History will be found a most excellent work for the ambitious student, who desires to undertake more advanced study.

Frequent references should be made to the musical map and the musical chart at the end of the book.

iii

CONTENTS.

APPENDIX.

STANDARD HISTORY OF MUSIC.

LESSON I.

HOW MUSIC BEGAN.

So FAR as our records go, all the people who lived long, long ago before the time of the birth of Christ showed a love for music. We are told that even among the savages

FIG. 1.—ANCIENT FORMS OF THE HARP, DRUM, FLUTE, AND CASTANETS.

of to-day there is always found some attempt to sing or to make some kind of musical sound. Music seems to be a part of man's nature, by which he expresses thoughts he would be unable to express through words, gestures, or by

means of writing, or the arts of painting, sculpture, etc.
The Chinese claim that music commenced in their country

Fig. 2.—Some Very Old Forms of the Harp in Ancient Egypt.

Fig. 3.—Performing on the Harp, from a Carving on the Tomb of an
Egyptian King.

three thousand years before the birth of Christ. Unfortunately, many records of the music of the older nations in the Far East have been lost, and our knowledge comes, for the most part, from carvings on monuments, which show that in India, Arabia, Babylonia, Assyria, Egypt, Persia and among the Hebrews, both instrumental and vocal music were known.

Fig. 4.—A Very Old Form of Drum.

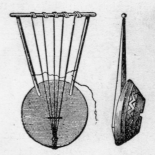

Fig. 5.—Ancient Hebrew Zither.

These carvings show wonderful pictures of the first musical instruments, which are particularly remarkable because our modern instruments of the harp, violin, guitar and drum families are much the same in principle. Figures 1 to 6 in-

Fig. 6.—Very Old Form of Egyptian Harp, Resembling our Modern Violin.

clusive are pictures of some of the instruments used. Note how they resemble modern instruments.

The first music of a nation or people was probably *Vocal* music and then the natural desire to tap *Time* regularly

(*Rhythm*) led to the making of instruments of wood, stone, metal, skin or clay for that purpose. Then, in order to have a system, *Scales* were discovered, and from these foundations the musical systems of all nations have sprung. The scales differed greatly. The Chinese, for instance, had a scale known to us as the *Pentatonic* (pent'-a-tonic) or *Five-Toned* scale, which sounded very much like this:

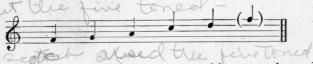

To each of these *Tones* they gave an odd name, thus: *Emperor, Prime Minister, Subject People, State Affairs,* and *Picture of the Universe.* Very strangely, the five-toned scale was used by the olden time musicians of Ireland and Scotland.

The Hindus divided the *Octave* into very small parts, and

THE GREEK LYRE.

had, it is said, thirty-six scales, although in their writings they speak of as many as sixteen hundred scales. What if one had to practice as many scales as that, instead of the twenty-four of which our own musical system is composed?

SAPPHO SINGING TO PHAON.

Showing the manner in which the Greek lyre was used.

It was, however, among the wonderful Greeks, who lived before the birth of Christ, that the foundations of our own kind of music were really laid. With them, poetry, art and culture were looked upon as real necessities, and the union of poetry with music made the study of the art of music one of great importance. At the performance of the famous Greek dramas, which were given in enormous open-air theatres, and attended by thousands, music was continually used and thus the people became familiar with it. One famous philosopher, **Terpander** (ter-pan'-der), born about 676 B. C., is said to have added three strings to the *Lyre* or Grecian harp, and another philosopher, **Pythagoras** (pi-thag'-o-ras), born about 582 B. C., is said to have added the eighth string.

Pythagoras also invented a system of four tones known as the *Tetrachord* (tet'-ra-kord) or series of four *Notes,* which led to the first scale of one octave. The following are tetrachords:

You will readily see how, when two tetrachords are arranged thus, an octave scale results.

They also had a *Chromatic* (kro-mat'-ik) scale, somewhat similar to our chromatic scale, and in time they built up a system of scales which was similar in many respects to a form of our modern *Minor* scales, called the *Normal* or the *Pure*. The Greek system as a whole was very hard to understand, but an idea of one part of it may be gained from the following:

Note that the normal Minor scale is the same as the *Major* scale of the same name, with the third, sixth and seventh steps of the scale lowered one-half tone, both going up and coming down the scale. The Greeks gave their scales odd names, such as *Dorian, Phrygian,* etc., as shown in the following:

1. *Dorian* (do'-re-an) scale, resembling the scale of D minor.

2. *Phrygian* (frig'-e-an) scale, resembling the scale of E minor.

3. *Lydian* (lid'-e-an) scale, resembling the scale of F sharp minor.

4. *Mixo-lydian* (mixo-lid'-e-an) scale, resembling the G minor scale.

5. *Hypo-dorian* (hi'-po-do'-re-an) scale, resembling the A minor scale. (Note the B flat introduced in this scale, which makes it different from the preceding scales.)

6. *Hypo-phrygian* (hi'-po-frig'-e-an) scale, resembling the B minor scale. (Similar in form to the Hypo-dorian.)

7. *Hypo-phrygian* (hi'-po-frig'-e-an) scale, resembling the C sharp minor scale. (Similar in form to the Hypo-dorian.)

The Greeks' scales were also called *Modes*.

You may see from the foregoing how important scales were considered thousands of years ago. It is not known that the Greeks practiced *Harmony,* or the art of combining sounds and *Chords* to produce beautiful effects. We must, however, be grateful to them for many of the terms used in modern music, as in modern medicine.

During the next one thousand years very little advance was made in musical art, except for the part played by the famous music workers of the early Church, and for the invention of a system of musical notation, without which future musical developments would not have been possible. Of these we shall learn in the following lessons.

TEN TEST QUESTIONS.

1. How long ago do the Chinese believe that music commenced?
2. Name eight nations in the Far East in which music was known.
3. What types of instruments were used by ancient peoples?
4. How many notes were in the Chinese scale?
5. What other nations used a similar scale?
6. How many scales are the Hindus said to have used?
7. How did the people of ancient Greece become familiar with music?
8. What is a tetrachord?
9. What modern scale does the old Greek scale resemble?
10. How many scales (or modes) did the ancient Greeks use?

LESSON II.

WHAT THE EARLY CHURCH DID FOR MUSIC.

DURING the one thousand years following the birth of Christ, the art, poetry and music of the world were closely connected with the efforts of the Church to bring the nations of Europe from pagan beliefs to the Christian religion. The seat of the Church was first in Rome, and then in Con-stan-ti-no'-ple, and again in Rome. Because of this Italian influence most of the musical terms we use to-day, *Allegro* (al-leh'-gro), *Andante* (ahn-dahn'-tay), *Legato* (lay-gah'-toh), etc., come from the Italian language.

Great cathedrals were built and the ablest artists and sculptors decorated them. Naturally, the foremost thinkers and musicians of the day gave their best to the Church. Tradition tells us that **Pope Sylvester** established the first school for the training of church singers in 330, A. D. **Ambrose, Bishop of Milan,** is said to have invented one set of scales and to have done much to promote musical art, but, as in the case of the famous **Pope Gregory I** (called "The Great"), who lived in the sixth century and who is said to have invented another set of scales, there is so very little that we know to be exact that it is unsafe to make positive statements. We do know, however, that the Church leaders did everything in their power to bring out the best in education, art, poetry and music, and that the most important work in music during these years was done under the influence of the Church.

GREGORIAN (GREH-GO'-RI-AN) MODES.

The Church also preserved the best in Greek learning, and it is not surprising that the scales invented should have been

designed after Greek models and have had similar names. However, owing to the fact that there had been no successful

2

means of writing down musical sounds (*Notation*), these Church scales, sometimes called modes, were mistaken imitations, and are thought by some not to be so good, from the standpoint of musical science, as the Greek scales. The accompanying table shows the points of difference.

Although these notes here given are in the form of the scale, they were not always employed in this order in actual musical work.

Note that, as we have said, the Greek scale was a kind of minor scale resembling the major scale of the same name, with the third, sixth and seventh degrees *Flatted*. Now note that the Church scales are all simple series of notes from one note to its octave above, just as they would be if played entirely without the use of any of the black keys on the pianoforte. We have seen in the first lesson how the root of the Greek system was a series of four tones, known as a tetrachord. In the eleventh century the Church fathers invented a system of six tones, known as the *Hexachord* (hex'-a-kord) system. This was applied to an old Latin hymn, the first syllable of each line of which commenced on a tone a step higher than the foregoing one, and from this we have derived the system of *Sol-fa* singing or *Solfeggio* (sol-fay'-gee-oh) used to-day. The hymn was:

> *Ut* queant laxis (Ut later changed to do).
> *Re*-sonare fibris (re).
> *Mi*-ra gestorum (mi).
> *Fa*-muli tuorum (fa).
> *Sol*-ve polluti (sol).
> *La*-bii reatum (la).
> *San*-cte Johannes (si), later changed by some to Te.

Ut queant la - - - xis Re - so - na - re fi - bris Mi - - - ra
ges - - to-rum Fa - mu-li tu - - o - rum Sol - - - ve pol-lu-ti
La - bi - i re - a - - - tum Sanc - - te Jo - an - nes.

The music that was sung in the churches during all these years has come to be called the *Gregorian style* or *Plain*

ST. AMBROSE.   POPE GREGORY I.

Song, and was supposed to have been originated by Pope Gregory I. Many do not believe this, and say that the name came from **Gregory II** or **Gregory III**, who lived in the eighth century. The Gregorian melodies were very many and varied, some six hundred being connected with the Mass and leading services of the Church. The notes had no set length, but usually followed the Latin words, as in a chant. The melodies were unaccompanied by harmony, and rarely went beyond the limits of one octave. The Gregorian style is the sole music ordered by the present **Pope Pius X** for regular use in the Church. Properly rendered, the Gregorian melodies are stately and beautiful. The following is part of a Gregorian melody of great age, used in the churches to-day.

This is a selection from the first movement of the Church Mass, called the *Kyrie,* and corresponds to the answer to the commandments in the Episcopal service, "Lord, have mercy upon us." Play the whole notes four times as long as written, the half notes four times as long as written and the black notes without stems (which were derived from the diamond-shaped notes of the old Gregorian notation), as long as whole notes. This value of the notes is by no means exact, but will give an idea of the stately manner in which the plain song was rendered. Until the sixteenth century *Bars* were not used except to show where breath should be taken.

In our next lesson we shall learn how the way to write music was invented, for this was more important to the future of the art than anything done in the thousand years we have been studying.

TEN TEST QUESTIONS.

1. With what body was music most closely connected during the first one thousand years after Christ?

2. Why do most of the musical terms we use to-day come from the Italian language?

3. What Pope is said to have established the first training school for singers?

4. What Bishop and what Pope are said to have devised scales?

5. How was Greek learning preserved?

6. How do the Church modes differ from the Greek modes (or scales)?

7. What is a hexachord?

8. From what do the syllables do, re, me, fa, sol, la, etc., come?

9. What is the Plain Song or Gregorian style, and who was supposed to have invented it?

10. What is the sole style of music ordered for regular use in the Catholic Church of to-day by Pope Pius X?

LESSON III.

HOW THE SYSTEM OF WRITING NOTES WAS INVENTED.

WHEN you look at the *Staff, Clefs* and *Notes,* used as signs for musical sounds, they seem very simple, but it took hundreds of years before this system of writing notes to represent music was completed. The oldest way of writing music by means of signs is credited to **Alypius** (al-ip'-i-us), who lived in Alexandria about 360, A. D. (many different dates are given by different authorities). He is said to have used the letters of the alphabet placed in different positions to represent different sounds.

In the sixth century **Boethius** (bo-e'-thi-us), a Roman philosopher, devised a system of giving each note, from the low *A* on the *Bass Clef* to the *A* on the *Treble Clef,* a separate letter of the alphabet, thus:

Later, smaller letters were used for the *Upper Notes.*

The next step was the invention of a kind of musical shorthand, the signs used being called *Neumes* (nu'-mes). There were from seven to forty of these signs used and they were placed over the syllables to be sung in such a way that the singer had to judge how high or how low the sound (*Pitch*) was, by the distance the sign was from the syllables. The following is a line of a Latin hymn with the neumes above:

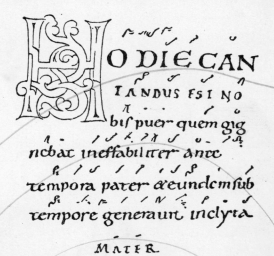

AN OLD LATIN MANUSCRIPT ACCOMPANIED BY SIGNS CALLED "NEUMES," USED
TO REPRESENT MUSICAL SOUNDS.

The little marks over the words are the neumes. The above is a facsimile of the handwriting of **St. Galen** (gah'-len), a monk who lived in the tenth century.

A little later the plan of showing the pitch by placing the words on parallel lines similar to the following was invented:

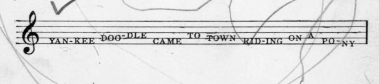

This served to show in a clumsy way how high or how low were the sounds accompanying the syllables, but it was not exact, nor did it show how long the sounds should be nor the key of the composition. The first known use of parallel lines in music is found in the writings of the monk **Hucbald** (huck'-bald), who lived in the ninth and tenth centuries.

Gradually a system was formed in which the neumes, or note-signs, were combined with the parallel lines. The next step was an attempt to show the pitch (the highness or the lowness of the tones) by means of colored lines. It is said that **Guido d'Arezzo** (gwee'-do dar-rayt'-zo), a famous teacher, singer and monk, who lived in the eleventh century, made a four-line staff, F being placed upon a red line, C on a yellow line, and A and E on black lines.

Important as this step was, the invention of the clefs to show the lines was more important. The clefs we use now are really nothing more than forms of old Latin letters. The following shows how the F, or bass clef, came into existence:

The following is a cut of how the G, or treble clef, came into existence:

All that was needed to complete this system were note-signs to indicate the length of the sounds. **Franco of Cologne** (frahn'-ko), a monk who lived in the twelfth century, is usually given the credit of inventing these, although we are by no means certain that he did anything more than write down the discoveries of other church writers who came before him. The first notes, showing the length of sounds, looked like the following:

It was not until the fifteenth century, however, that notes were invented with round shapes like our half notes and whole notes. With these came the invention of bars to show measures, and the main features of musical notation were complete. These inventions were of vast importance, and we shall see in the next lesson how they influenced the music of the following centuries.

Many different systems of writing music have been invented. One in particular, called the *Tonic-sol-fa,* in which the musical sounds were expressed by means of the letters of the alphabet, came into wide use in England and in parts of the United States in the nineteenth century. For general use, however, no system has ever been devised that has met with such wide and continued use as that of the five-line staff and the measured notes. In England our whole note is called a *semi-breve;* the half note, a *minim;* the quarter note, a *crochet;* the eighth note, a *quaver;* the sixteenth note, a *semi-quaver;* the thirty-second note, a *demi-semi-quaver.* This system is obviously much more likely to confuse the pupil than that generally employed in this country.

In orchestral *scores* or arrangements of the parts for the different instruments of the orchestra another clef may be noticed. This is called the *C clef,* and the line upon which it is placed becomes middle "C." It sometimes appears upon the first line, sometimes upon the third line and at other times upon the fourth line of the staff, being called the *soprano clef,* the *alto clef,* the *tenor clef* respectively.

TEN TEST QUESTIONS.

1. How long did it take before our way to write music was discovered?
2. Who was the celebrated Greek who used letters of the alphabet to represent musical sounds?
3. What did Boethius do?
4. What was the system known as neumes?
5. Who was the monk who first used parallel lines in music writing?
6. What important improvement did Guido d'Arezzo make?
7. From what do the G and the F clefs come?
8. Who is said to have invented notes having shapes indicating the length of sounds?
9. In what century were notes with round shapes invented?
10. What body of men must we thank for the invention of the art of writing music?

shirly the diffrence between them and what they are

LESSON IV.

WHO THE TROUBADOURS WERE AND WHAT THEY DID.

WE HAVE learned that during the first one thousand years after the birth of Christ, the leading musical work of the world was done under the shadow of the Church. Now, let us study the music of the next five hundred years and we shall learn of one of the most interesting and romantic times in the history of the art, for instead of being used solely for religion, music came to be used for love-songs, and to help in telling the tales of bravery and valor of the knights of old.

In the twelfth century, when chivalry was at its height and people lived a kind of story-book life, noble knights, men of wealth, and even kings, wrote poems and composed melodies, which were usually in praise of some lady fair. They then wandered from place to place singing them in the courts of castles or like serenades under some fair maiden's balcony window. They were called *Troubadours* (troo'-ba-door) or *Trouvères* (troo'-vairs). These names simply meant discoverers of new melodies or poems. The poet-singers of Southern France, then known as Provence, were called troubadours, while those of Northern France (Brittany and Normandy) were called trouvères. The songs of the troubadours were almost solely love-songs, while those of the trouvères were often upon old legends or myths or upon the deeds of some famous hero, such as the great emperor **Charlemagne** (sharl'-mayne), who at one time ruled almost all of Eastern Europe.

The melodies of the troubadours differed from the
Gregorian melodies of the Church, and it is thought by many
that some of them formed the basis for the *Folk-songs,* or

MONUMENT TO THE FAMOUS MEISTERSINGER, HANS SACHS, IN THE CITY OF
NUREMBURG, GERMANY.

Sachs was a shoemaker and a poet as well.

people's songs, of the French people of to-day.   To accompany their singing these poet-singers used instruments that
could be carried with them, such as the harp, the lute and the
viol.   Sometimes, when a troubadour was unable to compose

or play, he employed a *Joglar* (zhog'-lar), or *Jongleur* (zhong'-ler), who would serve him for pay. These joglars were often singers, acrobats, dancers or magicians, and our modern word *Juggler* comes from this source.

THE MINNESINGERS.

The troubadours of Germany were called **Minnesingers.** The word *Minne* (min'-neh) means love, so the word minne-singer means love-singer. Their songs gave more attention

Song.

Supposed to have been written by King Thibaut of Navarre (1201–1253)

to the beauty of nature and to religion than those of the troubadours. At first the melodies resembled the Gregorian style, but later they took on a more modern form. The minnesingers did not employ joglars, but sang and played their own songs. There is a tradition that in 1207 a great contest of minnesingers was held in the glorious old castle of the *Wartburg* (vart'-boorg), in a part of Germany known

PROCESSION OF MINNESINGERS.

as Thüringia (tier-ing'-i-a). The great composer **Richard Wagner** (reekh'-art vahg'-ner), of whom we shall learn later, made this song contest the scene for the second act of his opera *Tannhäuser* (tann'-hoys-er) and the Tannhäuser march, played so frequently, is the music used in the opera during the entrance of the singers in the great castle hall of the Wartburg, before the contest.

THE MEISTERSINGERS.

After the minnesingers in Germany came the **Meister-singers** (meys'-ter-sing-ers) or **Mastersingers.** These were mostly tradespeople and workmen who loved singing and enjoyed banding together for mutual pleasure. They formed clubs with formal rules and grades of membership from the beginner or *Scholar* class up to the full member or master-singer. Great contests were held in which many societies took part, just as is done in our modern *Sängerfests* (sen'-ger-fests) or song festivals held by Germans in Germany and in America.

The first club or guild of meistersingers is said to have been formed in Mayence (Germany) in 1300, and the last one remained until 1836 in the German city of Ulm. One of the famous meistersingers was **Hans Sachs** (sahks), a shoemaker of Nüremberg (neerm'-bairg), whom Richard Wagner has made the leading character in his opera, *Die Meistersinger*. The meistersingers, minnesingers, troubadours and trouvères were a kind of bridge from the Church music of the past to the music that was to follow, which we shall study in the following chapters.

The festivals held by the *Meistersingers* were made great

events.   This is indicated in Wagner's music-drama *Die Meistersinger,* when *Veit Pogner,* the rich goldsmith, offers his daughter *Eva,* together with his wealth as one of the prizes. Wagner also shows us how ridiculous were many of the rules laid down by the *Meistersingers.*

Although the *Meistersingers* went out of existence in 1836, the spirit still exists and the song festivals and conventions of music workers now held in all parts of the world are in a sense nothing other than a continuation of the old *Meistersinger* idea.

TEN TEST QUESTIONS.

1. What do the words "troubadour" and "trouvère" mean?
2. How did the troubadours differ from the trouvères?
3. Are the French folk-songs of the day believed to have come in part from the songs of the troubadours?
4. What instrument did the troubadours play?
5. What were the joglars or jongleurs?
6. What were the troubadours of Germany called?
7. What great contest of singers was supposed to have been held in the thirteenth century?
8. What were the meistersingers?
9. When was the first guild of meistersingers formed?
10. What was the name of the famous shoemaker meistersinger of Nüremberg, whom Richard Wagner has made the central character in his opera called Die Meistersinger?

LESSON V.

WHAT POLYPHONIC MUSIC WAS AND HOW IT CAME TO BE.

THUS far we have studied only music that consisted of a single series of notes or melody. This kind of music was called *Monophonic* (mon-o-fon'-ik), or one-voiced, from the Greek words *monos,* meaning one, and *phone,* meaning sound. The following is an example of monophonic music. Ex. I.:

Although this melody has an accompaniment, the accompaniment does not bring in any new melody, and therefore there is really only one melody, and the music is monophonic.

3   33

We shall now commence the study of music called *Polyphonic* (pol-e-fon'-ik), or many-voiced, from the Greek words *polus,* meaning many, and *phone,* meaning sound. The foregoing shows how two or more entirely different melodies may be combined. (See Ex. II.)

The science of combining melodies in this manner is called *Counterpoint,* which means point against point, or note against note. If the melody was accompanied by chords in the following manner it was said to be harmonized, and the science of doing this was called *Harmony.* Ex. III.:

Andante con moto.   MENDELSSOHN.

III.   etc.

We know that Hucbald, of whom we have already studied, wrote in two parts, in a manner called *Organum, Descant* (or-gan'-um des'-cant) or *Diaphony* (de-af'-o-ny), as early as the tenth century. The parts, however, often moved in parallel lines five degrees apart, in this manner:

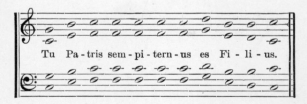

Tu Pa - tris sem - pi - tern - us es Fi - li - us.

This sounds very disagreeable to our ears and is one of the first things forbidden in our modern books on harmony.

Play the above over on your piano and see how tiresome to your ear it soon becomes. It is said that Guido d'Arezzo, who invented the four-line staff, wrote in organum with four voices or parts.

During the thirteenth, fourteenth, fifteenth and sixteenth centuries, the interest in art, manufactures, poetry and music so greatly increased that there came a time in the last-named century, known as the *Renaissance* (re-nay-sahns'), or re-birth of the civilized world. The discovery of America by Columbus, in 1492; the invention of printing by Gutenberg (goo'-ten-berg), in 1440, and later (1476) the invention of music printing, seemed to awaken the world to new activities in a most remarkable manner. With this awakening came a similar activity among the musicians. We have space to consider only a few of the most-noted masters of the time.

John Dunstable (duns'-ta-ble), who died in 1455, is given the credit of beng the first *Contrapuntist* (kon-tra-poon'-tist) ; that is, he is said to have written the first polyphonic music. Dunstable was born in England and was also a famous mathematician and astrologer. His music was known all over the western part of the European continent.

Guillaume Dufay (gwee-ome' duh-fay'), who was born at Hainaut (ay-no'), Belgium, and died in 1474, improved musical notation and developed what is known in music as the *Canon*. The canon is a form of music in which a given melody is accompanied a short distance later by an exact repetition of the same melody. An illustration of this is the old four-part canon, known as *Sumer is icumen in.* Many believe this to be the oldest known example of polyphonic music. It is in the British Museum in London, and was supposed to have been written at Reading Abbey about 1240, although many think that the writing shows that it was composed at a much later date.

Another famous composer of this wonderful time was **Jean de Okeghem** (zhang deh ok´-eg-hem), who was born in Flanders and died in 1495, and was known as the "Prince of Music." He was employed by three kings, one after the other, and made Paris the musical capital of Europe during his lifetime. He wrote twenty masses and many other compositions which place him far above all other musicians of his day.

Josquin Deprès (zhos-kan´ deh-pray), was born in France and died in 1530. He was a pupil of Okeghem and held many important musical posts in Paris and Rome. His compositions were very numerous and in many different styles. He was also a very great teacher.

Adrian Willaert (will´-aert), born at Bruges (breezh) and died in 1562. He first studied law in Paris, but then became a pupil of Deprès. In 1527 he became choirmaster of the great Cathedral of St. Mark's, in Venice, and in this position became very famous. He had many important pupils and wrote *Masses, Motets* (mo-téts) and *Madrigals* in great number. The motet was usually a sacred part-song, while the madrigal was a non-sacred part-song.

Orlando di Lasso (or-lan´-do de lahs´-so), or Orlandus Lassus, who, born at Mons (Hainaut) and died in 1594, was unquestionably one of the greatest musicians of his time. He had a remarkable voice as a boy, and because of this he was taken on frequent trips to foreign countries. He became court choirmaster in Munich (Germany) and made his choir famous throughout Europe. He wrote in almost every musical form then existing and his published compositions

number over twenty-five hundred.   Some of them are rendered by choral societies of this day, as are the madrigals,
masses and motets of other composers who lived in di Lasso's
time.   The most prominent person of these centuries, however, was the great Italian reformer, **Palestrina,** of whom we
shall learn in the next lesson.

TEN TEST QUESTIONS.

1. Of what does a melody consist?
2. What is music consisting of a single series of notes called?
3. What does the word "polyphonic" mean?
4. What is the art of combining melodies called?
5. What do we mean by harmony?
6. What was organum descant or diaphony?
7. Who is given the credit for writing the first polyphonic music?
8. Tell something of Dufay, Deprès and Willaert.
9. Who was Orlando di Lasso?
10. Are the works of the composers we have studied ever rendered
to-day?

LESSON VI.

WHO PALESTRINA WAS AND WHAT HE DID.

ALTHOUGH, as we have noted, the influence of the troubadours, minnesingers and meistersingers was very great, the
influence of the Church upon music was still greater. This
reached its height in the works of **Giovanni Pierluigi**
(jo-van'-ee pee-air-loo-ee'-djhee), who was known as **Palestrina** (pah-les-tree'-neh), because he was born in 1526 (some
say in 1514 and others in 1515) in the little Italian village
of Palestrina, near Rome.

The reason usually given for Palestrina's greatness is that
prior to his time the compositions of the masters showed too
clearly the laws which governed their compositions. Such
laws are called technical laws. *Technic* is the scientific or
mechanical means used to secure an artistic result. It is like
the scaffolding a builder puts up in order to erect a building.
If the builder allowed the scaffolding to remain on a new
building we might say that the technical means disfigured
the artistic result. The composers who were before Palestrina seemed to think more of the scaffolding, or laws of
composition, than they did of the compositions themselves.
Palestrina knew the laws, but with him the beauty of a composition was the first thought.

At the age of fourteen, Palestrina went to Rome to study,
and in 1544 returned to his native village as an organist.
He married in 1547. Four years later he was called as
choirmaster to St. Peter's, the great Cathedral in Rome. In

1555 he was taken into the Pope's private chapel. A change of Popes occurred, and after six months' service Palestrina was dismissed, because of a rule against married singers. He

PALESTRINA.

then served in two other Roman churches and in 1565 was employed by the Pope to supply works for the Papal Chapel. In 1571 he was called back to St. Peter's, where he remained until his death, twenty years later. Palestrina is commonly called "the Savior of Church Music," and the story which

gave him that name is that during the middle of the sixteenth
century the music of the Church became much lowered by the
use of popular melodies and non-sacred words in connection
with church music. This custom became so bad that a body
of church fathers, known as the "Council of Trent," prohibited
the use of anything but the Gregorian style or plain-song.
In 1564 **Pope Pius IV** called together a body of Cardinals
to reconsider the matter, with a view to admitting the works
of more modern composers. He recommended a mass by
Palestrina, known as the *Mass of Pope Marcellus,* because
Pope Marcellus had done much to make church music
better. Many authorities, however, deny that Palestrina
played a very important part in this controversy, although his
greatness was acknowledged by the Church.

Palestrina's works are all polyphonic and are very
numerous. The complete edition, now republished, makes
thirty-three large volumes. His works must be heard sung
by a choir of capable singers to be appreciated. Some of
his masses are still heard quite frequently in some foremost
Catholic churches. Palestrina died in 1594.

In the meantime a movement had arisen in Germany, known
as the "Reformation." The head of this movement was **Martin
Luther** (looth'-er), a monk who had been put out of the
Church because of his beliefs and because he objected to what
he thought were abuses in the Church System. Luther
believed that the music of the Church should be sung in the
language of the people, instead of in the Latin language.
Therefore he prepared a hymn-book which contained *Chorales*
or hymns, the melodies of which were either original or taken
from popular folk-songs. Luther was a musician and a performer on the flute and the lute, but he is not known to have

composed more than a few hymn-tunes. The one by which
he is best known is the fine old chorale, *Ein Feste Burg ist
unser Gott* (A strong fortress is our God). These chorales
had a very desirable effect in popularizing good music in Germany, as we shall learn in some later lessons.

A STRONG FORTRESS.

    This hymn has been credited to Martin Luther, although some authorities
contend that Luther wrote only the words of the hymn. It is a fine example
of the chorals which Luther made popular in Germany, and which are believed
to have had an important influence on music in that country.

TEN TEST QUESTIONS.

1. Why was Palestrina so called? *The town he was born in*
2. Why were the works of Palestrina considered greater than those of the composers who preceded him? *Guilty ? were won Shown to cleanly.*
3. How old was Palestrina when he went to Rome? *14.*
4. What important position did he hold in Rome? *Singer St Peter*
5. Why was plain-song the only kind of music ordered by the "Council of Trent?" *other was so bad, and got uncommon*
6. What was the name of the mass Palestrina wrote which led the Cardinals to reconsider the decision of the "Council of Trent?" *Mass of Pope Marc*
7. In what style are the works of Palestrina written? *Poly phonic*
8. In what language did Luther believe the church service should be sung? *Reformation.*
9. Of what kind of music was Luther's first hymn-book composed? *Choral*
10. Name a famous hymn by Martin Luther. *A Strong forte in our God,*

Tell who this King was ✓

LESSON VII.

WHAT EARLY ENGLAND GAVE TO MUSIC.

WE HAVE learned what had been done on the European continent during the first fifteen hundred years after the birth of Christ, but our history would be very incomplete if we did not study something of the works of the first composers of early England.   That music was known in early Ireland, Wales, Scotland and England there can be no doubt.   The stories of the musical *Bards* or poets are very many.   In the tenth century in Ireland the most famous musician was the **King Brian Boru,** and his harp with twenty-eight strings is to be seen in the Dublin Museum.   We have learned that the credit for the first polyphonic (many-voiced)writing was given to John Dunstable, who was an Englishman.   We have also learned that what is supposed to be the first example of polyphonic writing was the old English canon, *Sumer is icumen in.*

Thomas Tallis (or, as sometimes spelled, **Tallys**) was probably the most celebrated English musician after Dunstable.   He was born in 1520 and died in 1585.   He was organist at Waltham Abbey and at the Chapel Royal.   With his pupil Byrd he obtained a monopoly of the music-publishing business in England.   He left many remarkable choral works, which won him the title of "The Father of English Choral Music."   One of his hymn-tunes, known as *Tallis,* is still to be found in our hymnals.   The music of this hymn is:

43

A Hymn by Tallis, Frequently Used in Churches To-day.

William Byrd (born about 1543 and died in 1623) was a pupil of Tallis and became organist at Lincoln and later at the Chapel Royal. He wrote a great deal for the *Virginal,* which was a keyboard instrument with strings similar to the piano, but with a different method of sounding the strings. Byrd also wrote many masses, motets, anthems, psalms, madrigals and songs, and was thought by many in his own day to be equal to Palestrina and di Lasso.

John Bull (born 1563 and died 1628) became organist of the Chapel Royal in 1597 and later became professor of music at Gresham College. He was very famous as a *virtuoso* (veer-too-o'-so), and in 1617 became organist of the Cathedral in Antwerp. His polyphonic writing was considered excellent and he wrote many pieces for instruments with keyboards. The melody of "God Save the King," known in America as "My Country, 'Tis of Thee," is generally attributed to him.

Without question, however, the most famous composer of early England was **Henry Purcell,** who was born at London

HENRY PURCELL.

in 1658 and died in 1695, at the age of 37. His family was musical; he was left an orphan and entered the Chapel Royal as a choir-boy, serving under the famous organists, **Cooke, Humphrey** and **Blow.** In 1675 he set music to a play by **Tate,** which met with such immediate success that he continued to write other songs and music for plays with great rapidity. He wrote music for over forty plays and operas for which the leading poets of his day furnished the words. In 1680 he became organist at Westminster Abbey and two years later at the Chapel Royal. This turned his attention to composition for the Church, and he wrote over one hundred anthems, three services and numerous songs, etc. His music was very original, and for nearly two centuries his position as the greatest of all English musicians was not disputed by any. We have seen that Purcell wrote music for plays and operas. We shall learn, in the next chapter, of the first musical plays, and also of the kind of sacred musical dramas called *Oratorios* (or-a-to'-ri-os).

Another early English musician whose works have won enduring fame was **Henry Lawes** (1595-1662), who wrote the music to Milton's "Comus" and who was a great friend of the immortal epic poet. **Thomas Augustine Arne** (1710-1778) was the composer of "Rule Britannia" and some of the most vigorous as well as the most graceful English songs. He was a Doctor of Music of Oxford and wrote two oratorios, several operas and the music to some of the Shakespeare plays.

TEN TEST QUESTIONS.

1. Name a famous Irish king who is known as a musician.
2. To which country is given the credit of producing the first contrapuntal music?
3. Name a famous hymn by Thomas Tallis which is sung to-day.
4. What English musician was considered in his day as the equal of Palestrina?
5. What English musician was famed as an organist?
6. Who is thought to be the greatest of early English musicians?
7. For how many plays did Purcell write the music?
8. In what famous church was Purcell organist?
9. Did Purcell write music for the church service?
10. How long did Purcell hold his rank as the foremost musician of England?

LESSON VIII.

THE BEGINNINGS OF THE ORATORIO AND THE OPERA.

In Lesson I we learned how the Greeks used to give performances of plays, accompanied by music, in great, open-air theatres. In days when there were no newspapers to reach the masses of the public these plays were of great educational importance. People, in general, are more deeply moved by things they see acted before them than by things they read in print. Realizing this, the heads of the early Christian Church gave performances representing miracles and Bible stories. These were known as moralities, mysteries or miracle plays. *The Passion Play,* representing the life and crucifixion of Christ, given to this day at Ober-Ammergau (o-bair-am′-er-gow), in Bavaria, is a continuation of this custom. From these miracle plays came the opera and the oratorio, as well as our modern music drama.

Filippo Neri (nay′-ree), an Italian priest and educator, who died in 1595, formed the custom of having sacred words set to music sung after his addresses. He also founded a body of priests, known as the Congregation of the Oratory, in 1575. The services of this body were held in a part of the church known in Italian as the *oratorio,* or in English as the oratory. Later this brotherhood gave sacred musical plays, with and without acting, and these plays came to be known as oratorios. They were the forerunners of our modern oratorios, which

47

are sacred musical plays usually given by choruses, accompanied by an orchestra, with the assistance of a quartet of solo singers, who sing the parts of the leading characters. In the oratorio there is no scenery, as in the case of a play, and there is no acting, the singers standing in one position during the entire performance.

As early as 1575, in Florence, Italy, the Count of Vernio, **Giovanni Bardi** (bahr'-dee), who was a noble and cultured amateur poet and musician, gathered around him a number of amateur poets and musicians, who sought to revive the old Greek plays. The music of the Greeks had by this time become practically a lost art. The first attempts of this little body of art lovers were called *Monodies* (mon'-o-dies), and they were little more than stories or legends set to music with a simple accompaniment. This style was soon to be used in plays, and in 1594 two of these amateurs, named **Peri** (pay'-ree) and **Caccini** (cah-chee'-nee), wrote the music to a play called *Dafne* (daff'-neh), and thus produced what is known as the first opera. Several other composers contributed to this movement, among them **Galilei** (gal-e-leh'-e), the father of the great astronomer, but we have not space to consider them now. Several similar musical plays followed, and in 1600 a sacred musical play, by **Cavaliere** (cah-vahl-ee-air'-ee), called *The Representation of the Soul and the Body,* was given in Rome, and this is looked upon by some as the first oratorio, although it was only one of a series of oratorios given by the brotherhood of which we have spoken.

Had it not been for the great genius of **Claudio Monteverde** (mon-teh-vair'-dee), who was born in Cremona in 1567, and died in 1643, this new style might not have become so popular as it did. He was very bold in making changes which he believed improved the music for his texts, and soon realized that the polyphonic style of voice writing was not best for the dramatic style, and thus he returned to the monophonic style, which permitted of much greater freedom, since it had to do with a melody and its accompaniment. Most of his life was spent in Venice, and although he became choirmaster of the Cathedral of St. Mark's in that city in 1613, and wrote some sacred music, Monteverde devoted himself almost exclusively to dramatic music. The interest in his work spread throughout all Europe, and this led to the establishment of the world's first opera house in Venice, in 1637. Of the twelve operas he wrote, only four exist now, and of these *Orfeo* (or-fay'-oh) and *Arianna* (ah-ree-ah'-nah) are the most famous. The orchestra used to accompany these operas included as many as thirty-one instruments.

The work of Monteverde was continued by many able musicians and writers for the stage, chief among whom were **Francesco Cavalli** (cah-vah'-lee), died in 1676; **Marc Antonio Cesti** (chehs'-tee), died in 1669; **Giacomo Carissimi** (cah-rees-ee'-mee), died in 1674; **Emilio de Cavalieri** (cah-vah-lee-air'-ee), died in 1602, and **Alessandro Stradella** (strah-dell'-ah), died in 1681 (?). Interesting as were the works of these composers for the stage, they cannot be looked upon as of equal importance with those of Monteverde.

We shall learn in later chapters of the deep influence opera has had upon the work of famous composers. With very few exceptions most of the great masters have written operas. All have not been successful in writing operas which have added to their fame, but it should always be remembered that a large part of the success of an opera depends upon the words, which are known as the *book,* or the *libretto*. In the early operas

4

little attention was paid to the book, and as a result we find operas written as late as 1850 with books so absurd and crude that the very best music that could be written could not keep them alive.

A great improvement in the books of the operas came with the works of Richard Wagner, who wrote his own librettos. Wagner had a strong sense of what made the best impression upon the stage, and many of his librettos make good dramatic literature entirely apart from the music. In a little over three hundred years the opera has made great advances, and the magnificent performances given to-day cannot be in any way compared with those given under the direction of the composers described in this chapter.

TEN TEST QUESTIONS.

1. Why did the early Church leaders favor the giving of plays?
2. What were the first plays called?
3. Give a modern example of the Passion Play.
4. Who was the Italian priest who formed the Congregation of the Oratorio?
5. What noble amateur attempted to revive the old Greek plays with music?
6. What was the name of the first opera?
7. What was the name of the work known as the first oratorio?
8. To which great master did opera owe its great advance in the seventeenth century?
9. Was Monteverde's style monophonic or polyphonic?
10. Were the works of the other composers who lived at the same time as important as the operas of Monteverde?

LESSON IX.

ALESSANDRO SCARLATTI AND OTHER FAMOUS ITALIAN COMPOSERS OF THE EIGHTEENTH CENTURY.

WE HAVE already seen what a wonderful influence Italy had upon musical art, and before we turn our attention to the great masters of Germany and France, such as **Bach** (bahch), **Handel** (hand'-el), **Lully** (luh'-lee), and **Rameau** (rah'-mo), let us stop for a little while to learn of some of the other famous Italian composers.

In the early part of the eighteenth century the operatic centre, which had been in Venice, on the northeastern coast of Italy, moved to Naples, on the western coast of Italy. Without doubt the most famous of all composers of this new centre was **Alessandro Scarlatti** (skahr-lah'-tee), who was born in Sicily in 1659. He studied in Naples and in Rome and when he was only twenty-one years of age, produced an opera in the latter city. He held several important posts as choirmaster, and in Naples he taught in three conservatories. He was very gifted and not only composed and taught, but conducted, sang and played on the *Harpsichord* (harp'-see-kord), one of the forerunners of the piano. His work is said to have influenced that of the great German composer Handel, of whom we shall learn later. Scarlatti wrote over one hundred and fifteen operas, and the *Arias* (ah'-ree-ahs) or elaborated vocal solos from these operas are particularly beautiful. Scarlatti's writing for orchestral

instruments was also remarkable for its time.   He wrote
many oratorios, serenatas or serenades, madrigals and cantatas.   A *Cantata* is a kind of short oratorio and in our day
frequently has a subject that is not sacred.   Scarlatti taught
many famous pupils, one of whom was his son, **Domenico**

ALESSANDRO SCARLATTI.

Scarlatti, born in 1685 and died in 1757, who became very
famous as a performer on the harpsichord and the organ.
His compositions for the keyboard instruments showed great
originality and opened up many new ways of playing the
instruments.   In fact, the harpsichord compositions of Alessandro and Domenico Scarlatti are now published for the

modern pianoforte and some are quite frequently heard in concerts. They are very quaint and have a charm which many people enjoy greatly.

Of the other Italian composers of this time who were less celebrated than the Scarlattis, we have only space to consider a few. Niccolo Porpora (nik-ko-lo por'-poh-rah), born in Naples in 1686 and died in 1766, wrote successful operas, but was chiefly known as a singing teacher. Many of the most famous singers of the day were his pupils. In 1745 he located in Vienna as a teacher, and while there the great master Haydn (high'-dn), of whom we shall learn later, became his pupil.

Niccolo Jomelli (yo-mel'-ee), born near Naples in 1714 and died in 1774, wrote over forty-five operas and many religious works of high and stately character. He was considered by many equal to the greatest composers of his day.

Giovanni Battista Pergolesi (pair-go-lay'-zy), born near Naples in 1710 and died in 1736, was a composer whose works showed such charm of melody that many of his songs are sung to-day by great artists at song recitals. Although he died at an early age, from consumption, and wrote only fourteen operas and a few other compositions, his music is so simple, delicate and beautiful that it is much praised.

Other noted Italian composers and musicians of the day were Francesco Durante (fran-ches'-ko doo-rahn'-te), died in 1755; Nicola Piccinni (pit-chee'-nee), died in 1800; A. M. G. Sacchini (sah-kee'-nee), died in 1786; Giovanni Battista Bononcinni (bo-non-chee'-nee), died in 1750, and Giovanni Paisiello (pah-ee-see-el'-lo), died in 1816. Of these men and their music you should learn when you take up your studies in advanced musical history.

The influence of the works of the Scarlattis was felt for over two centuries. Alessandro Scarlatti was an imposing and charming man who made many friends and won for himself many important positions. For some years he was under the patronage of the Queen of Sweden, and later in life he was knighted by the Pope for his services to the art of church music. Domenico was so able a performer upon the harpsichord that he was considered the equal of Handel in a contest held to determine the ability of the two players. Handel, however, was regarded as a better organist than Domenico Scarlatti.

TEN TEST QUESTIONS.

1. What country had the greatest influence upon early musical art? *Italy*
2. Where was A. Scarlatti born? *Sicily*
3. What instrument did A. Scarlatti play? *Harpsichord.*
4. Which great composer was influenced by the works of Scarlatti? *Handel*
5. What is a cantata? *Not Sacred,*
6. What is an aria?
7. For what was Domenico Scarlatti famed? *As a performer on the Organ*
8. Which great Italian master was Haydn's teacher? *Niccolo Porpora*
9. Name four or five famous composers of the same period. *Italy*
10. To what particular form of the art did the great Italian masters give the most of their attention?

LESSON X.

THE WONDERFUL BACH FAMILY, AND SOME GERMAN MUSICIANS WHO LIVED AT THE SAME TIME.

WE HAVE found it necessary to mention the names of Bach and Handel several times. So great were these musicians that their work stands out more prominently than that of any of the musicians we have studied. We shall learn about them in the latter part of this history, which treats of the musicians who are generally classed as modern. Before this, however, let us study something of the wonderful **Bach** family and of the German musicians who lived about the same time.

For over two centuries the **Bach** (bahch) family, which came into existence in Thüringia, in the centre of Germany, was famous for the great number of its musicians. The first was **Hans Bach, of Wechmar,** who was supposed to have been born late in the sixteenth century. His son, **Veit Bach,** was born in 1619, and the family during the next eight generations produced no less than fifty-two musical members. Most of these musicians worked principally in sacred music and for the church organ, but many have written equally well in non-sacred styles and for other instruments than the church organ. The most famous members of the Bach family were:

Johann Christoph Bach, who was born in Arnstadt in 1642 and died in 1703. He was town organist for thirty-eight years in Eisenach, Germany, and was an original composer.

55

Johann Michael Bach, born at Arnstadt in 1648, died in 1694; a noted organist, composer and maker of instruments.

Johann Sebastian Bach, born in Eisenach in 1685 and died in 1750; the greatest of all the Bachs.

SCENE IN THE HOME OF JOHANN SEBASTIAN BACH.
Bach was married twice and had, it is said, twenty children in all.

Karl Philip Emanuel Bach, born in Weimer in 1714, died in 1788; son of the great Bach, and the foremost keyboard performer of his day.   He was also a composer of sacred choral works and wrote much for the *Clavier* (klah'-vee-eh).   His works for clavier laid the foundation for the *Sonata-form* (so-nah'-tah), of which we shall learn later, and greatly influenced the famous musician Franz Josef

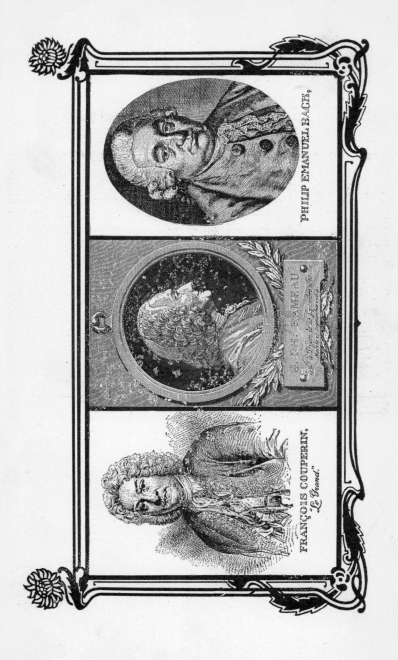

PHILIP EMANUEL BACH,

J. PH. RAMEAU

FRANÇOIS COUPERIN,
"Le Grand."

Haydn, who developed this form, and of whom we shall learn in the latter part of this history.

Of the other famous German musicians who lived about this time we can only consider the most prominent. **Johann Adolph Hasse** (has'-seh), born near Hamburg in 1699 and died in 1783; although a German, his style was so much like that of the Italians that he is frequently classed with them. The Bach family was for the most part devoted to Protestant church music. Hasse is famed for his Catholic church music, which is very melodious and strong. He traveled much over Europe and was popular at many courts. The number of his compositions is enormous. He wrote ten oratorios and about seventy operas, besides many other works.

Johann Joseph Fux (fooks), died in 1741; another German musician about whose early life little is known; he is principally interesting to us because he wrote a lengthy work on musical theory (harmony, counterpoint and composition) which remained as a guide to composers for nearly one hundred years. He wrote numerous compositions, including fifty-four masses, eight operas, two *Requiems* (a requiem is a part of the Catholic musical service used at funerals and in honor of the dead).

Heinrich Schütz (sheets), born in 1585 in Thüringia, exactly one hundred years before the great Bach, and died in 1672. He was first a choir-boy at Cassel, Germany, and later became a law student. His musical talent, however, was so great that he was sent by a nobleman to Venice to study. For nearly fifty-five years he was choirmaster at the leading church in Dresden. He wrote many excellent works, among which are some oratorios which have been particularly praised for their beautiful choruses. He taught several pupils who afterward became famous. His *Singspiel* (song-play) *Dafne,* produced in 1627, is called by some the first German opera. Unfortunately, the music of this work is lost.

TEN TEST QUESTIONS.

1. From what part of Germany did the Bach family come? *Thuringia*
2. Who was the first member of note? *Hans*
3. Who was the greatest member of the Bach family? *Veit*
4. Which member had much to do with laying the foundation for the modern sonata form? *Karl Philip Emanuel*
5. For what was Johann Hasse famed? *Catholic church music*
6. What was the principal work of Johann Joseph Fux? *Musical Theory —*
7. What is a requiem? *Part of Catholic music used for funerals —*
8. Who was Heinrich Schütz? *Choir boy later law student Choir master*
9. What work is called the first German opera? *Singspiel - Dafne,*
10. Name five prominent members of the Bach family.

Hans Bach.
Veit Bach —
Johann Christoph Bach —
Johann Michael Bach.
Johann Sebastian Bach.
Karl Philip Emanuel Bach —

LESSON XI.

MUSIC IN FRANCE IN THE SEVENTEENTH AND EIGHTEENTH CENTURIES.

WE HAVE learned something of the wonderful interest taken in music in Italy and in Germany, and now we shall study something of the works of some of the noted French composers who lived about the same time. For centuries the city of Paris had been the centre of learning, architecture and painting for men of wealth and leisure. The University of Paris was far-famed, and the rulers of the country, particularly the kings known as Louis XIV, Louis XV and Louis XVI, had spent money in the freest possible manner. This attracted art workers from all countries, and among them was **Jean Baptiste Lully** (zhon bap-teest lul'-lee), who, it is said, was born of noble parents in Florence, Italy, in 1633, and died in 1687. As a child he was taught the violin and the lute, and played so remarkably that he was taken to Paris by a French nobleman, the Duke of Guise. At first he was given a position as a kitchen boy, for we are still writing of the time when musicians were considered menials or servants. Lully's talent was so great that he was promoted to the band of King Louis XIV, and later became leader of the band and improved it very greatly. His success led to the position of court composer (in 1653) and his ability led to a firm friendship with the king. He wrote about fifteen operas, which won him wide fame. He also wrote many ballets, some church music

and numerous pieces for instruments of the violin and keyboard types. In 1681 he was made a noble and also court
secretary. Of his operas the following are the most famous:
Alceste (al-cest′), *Isis* (e′-sis), *Persee* (pehr′-zay) and *Armide*
(ar-mee′-deh). Extracts from these are heard at concert
programs of this day. Lully had a very bad temper, and in

LULLY PLAYING IN THE KITCHEN OF A NOBLEMAN.
Lully was brought from Italy to France as a scullion or kitchen-boy.

1687, when he was conducting a rehearsal of an orchestra, he
struck his foot so hard with his baton or conductors' stick,
which was then long, like a cane, that a disease set in which
caused his death.

François Couperin (fran-swah koop′-er-rang), born at
Paris in 1668 and died in 1733, was the most famous of a noted

family of organists and performers on the *Clavecin* (clah'-ve-
san), a keyboard instrument resembling the piano in some
ways. For over one hundred and fifty years, from 1650 to
1800, members of the family had been famous as musicians,
and each one of these musicians was in his time organist at the
Church of St. Gervaise, in Paris. The Couperin of whom we
write was the most famous of his family and was known as
"Couperin the Grand." He became organist in the king's
private chapel and wrote several excellent collections of pieces
for the clavicin, many of which are now performed on the
pianoforte. He also wrote, in 1717, one of the first instruction books for the keyboard instruments which preceded the
piano. His pieces were marked by what is known as *Embellishments,* such as *Grace Notes, Turns* and *Trills,* and his
style was widely imitated by other composers who followed
him. His pieces were grouped in sets or *Ordres,* and this
arrangement led to what later became known as the *Suite*
(sweet). A suite is a collection of short pieces, usually
dances, to be played one after the other and so arranged that
the contrast between the pieces adds to the beauty of the
group. The suite was one of the forerunners of the sonata,
about which we shall learn more later on.

After Lully and Couperin, the most prominent French
musician of his time undoubtedly was **Jean Philippe Rameau**
(rah'-mo). He was born at Dijon (de'-zhon), France, in
1683, just two years before the birth of the famous German
musicians, Bach and Handel, of whom we are to hear so much
later. Rameau was known as a *Prodigy;* that is, he showed
his musical talent at a very early age. At seven he played
the clavier, one of the forerunners of the piano. His early
training was excellent and at the age of eighteen he became

famous as an organist and was sent to Italy for further study. The music of Italy, however, did not appeal to him and he returned to France, playing for a time as violinist in a traveling opera company and later becoming an organist. His greatest triumphs were achieved in Paris from 1733 to his death in 1764. Here he produced many famous operas, one of which, *Hippolyte et Aricie* (hip-po-leet' eh ar-ee-see), has recently been reproduced at the Grand Opera in Paris. Rameau became a rival to Lully, and many think him far greater as a musician, although his music was not considered as dramatic; that is, as well suited for the stage as that of Lully. Rameau died in 1764.

We have now studied the lives of the more prominent musicians who preceded, and of those who lived at the same time as, the great masters, Bach and Handel. Before proceeding to the study of these great men, let us see in the following lesson how much the development of the instruments had to do with the progress of music.

TEN TEST QUESTIONS.

1. Why did Paris become a musical centre? *A Lot of Money Spent on it*
2. Where was Lully born? *Florence Italy*
3. What was the reason he came to France? *As a Kitchen boy.*
4. What king made Lully his friend? *King Louis 14.*
5. Are Lully's works played to-day? *Yes. —*
6. What was the singular cause of Lully's death? *Stamped foot too hard*
7. Who was "Couperin the Grand"? *Noted organ performer —*
8. What is a suite? — *Grace notes, turns & trills.*
9. Tell something about Rameau. *was known as a Prodigy.*
10. What is a prodigy?

LESSON XII.

HOW THE ORGAN, THE VIOLIN AND THE PIANO INFLUENCED THE ART OF MUSIC.

THUS far we have studied about the men who have made music, and now we shall see how the principal musical instruments of the time influenced musical art.

No one knows just when the **Organ** came into existence, but we do know that it was used in churches in the thirteenth century and that the early builders were monks. Besides the organs used in the churches, there were also smaller organs, called *Positives, Portatives* or *Regals,* which could be used in private houses or carried in the frequent church processions in the streets. These smaller organs are considered by many as more important than the larger instruments, as in the home many styles of music could be played that would not be allowed in the church.

In the sixteenth and seventeenth centuries, organ builders who were not monks made some remarkable instruments. The organs were made right in the churches, and not partly in factories, as is done now. The most famous organists of the fifteenth and sixteenth centuries were **Adrian Willaert** (ah'-dree-an vill'-ehrt), about whom we have already studied; **Girolamo Frescobaldi** (fres-co-bal'-dee), born in Ferrara in 1583 and died in 1644, who as organist of St. Peter's, in Rome, became one of the most famous players of his day; **Johann J. Frohberger** (fro'-behr-gehr.), died in 1667, a pupil

of Frescobaldi, who became organist to the Emperor of
Austria; **Dietrich Buxtehude** (dee'-trich bux-te-hoo'-deh),
born in Denmark in 1637, or, according to some, 1609, and
died in 1707. Buxtehude was the greatest organ performer
of his day. He was also the composer of many valuable
organ works. The musical vespers he conducted at his church
at Lübeck (lee'-beck) made him known throughout Europe.

BIBLE REGAL.
An early form of portable organ.

As we have seen in Lesson I, some of the most ancient
instruments of the countries of the Far East resembled the
violin in shape. It was, however, not until after the middle
of the sixteenth century that the **Violin,** as we know it, came
into being. In the parts of northern Italy known as Brescia
(breh'-sha) and Cremona (kray-mo'-na), many devoted
workers labored during a century and a half to make the
best violins possible. These workers were mostly in family
groups and may be classified by their first known members

5

ANTONIO STRADIVARI.

The workshop of the great violin-maker.

study about Violin

thus: **Andrea Amati** (ah-mah'-tee), of Brescia, died in 1577; **Gasparo da Salo** (sah'-lo), of Brescia, died in 1609; **Giovanni Paolo Maggini** (mad-jee'-nee), of Brescia, died about 1640; **Antonio Stradivari** (strah-dee-vah'-ree), of Cremona, died in 1737; **Pietro Andrea Guarneri** (gwar-neh'-ree), of Cremona, died in 1695; **Jakob Stainer** (stine'-er), born in the Tyrol (tee-rol) and died in 1683.

The improvement of the violin naturally produced greater composers for the instrument, and **Archangelo Corelli** (cor-reh'-lee), who was born in Italy in 1653 and died in 1713, won great fame as a violinist, teacher and composer. He wrote pieces divided into several parts, which were to be played upon one, two, or, in some cases, three instruments. These were called *Church Sonatas,* the word sonata coming from the Italian word *Suonare,* meaning "to sound." Later this form was developed into a style of composition that has since been used by most of the great composers.

After Corelli, the most famous violin master was **Giuseppe Tartini** (tar-tee'-nee), who died in 1770. As a composer and as an originator of ideas and methods of violin playing, he stands alone. In 1728 he established a famous school of violin playing and taught many successful pupils. His violin sonata called *The Devil's Trill* is still played by our great violinists.

We now come to stringed instruments of the keyboard class. At first strings were stretched over a hollow body of well-seasoned wood, to increase the sound, and these strings were either picked, as in the case of the *Zither,* or the strings were sounded by blows from rods or hammers, as in the case of the *Dulcimer* (dul'-ci-mer). The first keyboard instruments were called *Clavichord*s (klav'-i-kords) or *Claviers* (klah'-veers), and were somewhat similar to the dulcimer with a keyboard attached, which operated the striking rods or, as they were then called, *Tangents*. These tangents were made of brass, and when they struck the string they remained on it and did not rebound, as do the hammers of our modern piano.

The earliest clavichords (sixteenth century) had only twenty keys, and in the eighteenth century there were but fifty. The modern pianoforte has eighty-eight notes or keys. The tone of the clavichord was very thin and wiry. It was sweet and tinkling, but weak and short. In fact, the tone could only be prolonged by a kind of *Tremolo* (treh'-mo-lo) or, as it was

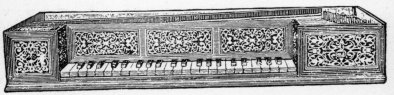

KEYBOARD OF AN INSTRUMENT OF THE SPINNET AND CLAVICORD TYPE.

then called, *Bebung*. This is one of the reasons we find so many trills, graces or embellishments in the music of the early classical composers.

The successor of the clavichord was the *Harpsichord,* in which the strings were picked by little quills worked from a keyboard. The tone in some cases was more powerful than that of the clavichord, but it was difficult to make the tone louder or softer.

The instrument that was to enable the player to make tones both loud and soft and which, in fact, was first called the **Fortepiano** (for-te-pee-ah'-no) and later the **Pianoforte** (from the two Italian words, *forte,* meaning *loud,* and *piano,* meaning *soft*), was invented by **Bartolommeo Christofori** (bar-to-lo-meh'-o krees-toh-foh'-ree) in Florence, about 1687. Some authorities give the date 1711, or the first time the piano-forte was mentioned in printed accounts. In the piano the string was struck by a hammer which immediately rebounded from the string. From this has come our modern piano. The instruments were first triangular, then square, then upright in shape. The piano is considered a vast improvement on the clavichord and the harpsichord.

TEN TEST QUESTIONS.

1. When was the organ first known? *No one knows but it was played in the Churches in the 13th century*
2. Who were the first organ builders? *monks*
3. Name three famous organists of the seventeenth century. *Adrian Willaert Frescobaldi Frongley*
4. When did the violin in its modern form come into existence? *16th Century*
5. What parts of Italy were famed for famous violin-makers?
6. Name four famous violin-makers. *Brescia Cremona*
7. Who were Tartini and Corelli? *teachers of violin and organ*
8. What was the first ancestor of the piano called? *Clavichord*
9. Who made the first pianoforte?
10. Why is the pianoforte called a pianoforte? *From the Italian word forte meaning loud and piano meaning soft.*

Johann Sebastian Bach.

LESSON XIII.

JOHANN SEBASTIAN BACH, THE GREATEST OF POLYPHONISTS.

WE HAVE now traced the history of music from its earliest beginnings up through the music of Greece and of the early Christian Church, and through the music of the troubadours, through the Middle Ages to the eighteenth century; but because of their great influence we have reserved two special lessons for the two masters, Bach and Handel, who were both born in 1685 in German cities only a few miles apart.

Johann Sebastian Bach (bahch) a member of the famous Bach family we have already studied, was born in Eisenach and was the son of an able violinist, Ambrosius Bach. At ten he became an orphan and was taken into the home of his brother Christoph, organist at Ohrdorf. His father had taught him the violin and his brother taught him the harpsichord and the organ. At Ohrdorf he went to school, and his fine boy-soprano voice was highly appreciated there. At fifteen he secured a position in the choir and school of St. Michael's (Mish'-ayl's) at Lüneberg (leeneh-berg), near the city of Hamburg. When his child voice changed to that of the man, his ability to play saved him his position. The organist at Lüneberg was Georg Bohm, and with his assistance and that of an excellent library of church music, Bach advanced greatly. In Hamburg and Celle he heard much good music and made up his mind early to devote himself to church music. Three years later he secured a position

71

as violinist at Weimar (vy'-mar), but soon thereafter was made town organist at Arnstadt. Here he had a fine new organ and began his work in musical composition.

BIRTHPLACE OF BACH IN EISENACH.

Bach spent most of his life within a comparatively few miles of this house.

Bach's desire to improve himself led him to walk over two hundred miles to Lübeck (lee'-beck), where he could hear the famous organist Buxtehude. His enthusiasm led him to overstay his leave of absence, and he went to Mühlhausen (meel'-how-zen), where he made many improvements in the music and the service. Here also he married his cousin, Maria Bach. His fame was now growing very rapidly and he was soon called to Weimar as court organist and violinist to the duke.

Bach remained in Weimar about nine years, and here he advanced greatly, both as a performer on the organ and as a composer. Now and then he would go to neighboring cities, such as Leipzig (lipe'-sik) and Halle (hal-leh), to examine the organs. He also made himself familiar with the works of the great Italian, Frescobaldi. He wrote cantatas for the church, suites for clavichord and harpsichord, and many fugues. A *Fugue* (fewg) is a kind of musical composition in which the first melody or *Subject* is continually repeated and imitated on different degrees of the scale throughout the entire composition. The word fugue is thought by some to come from a Latin word meaning *flight,* because the subject seems to fly through the entire work.

Bach is known as the great master of the fugue, and he wrote great numbers of them for the organ and the piano, many of them still being played by pianists and organists.

Bach's next position was at Cöthen (kay'-ten), where, owing to religious conditions, the organ had but little part in the church service. Therefore he gave more attention to the other instruments, particularly to the clavichord and the harpsichord. While at Cöthen he frequently visited Halle, Handel's birthplace, although he never met the great master.

In 1720 Bach's first wife died, and one year later he married at Weissenfels (vise'-sen-fels) Anna Wilken, a beautiful and accomplished singer, who helped him greatly in his work. Bach had in all twenty children.

In 1723 Bach went to Leipzig as *Cantor* (kan'-tor) or musical director of the Thomasschule (St. Thomas' School) and remained there until he died of apoplexy in 1750. One year before his death he became totally blind. In Leipzig Bach wrote many church cantatas and oratorios, including five *Passions,* or oratorios, dealing with the last hours of Christ. His *Christmas Oratorio* is also very famous. His published works comprise fifty large volumes.

Bach was robust in appearance and dignified in manner, yet kindly and good-humored. Aside from being the greatest of all masters of polyphony, he was also an excellent organ builder and a good music engraver.

TEN TEST QUESTIONS.

1. Where was Bach born? *Eisenach.*
2. Was his father musical? *Yes - Violinist*
3. Tell something of his musical boyhood. *An orphan at 10 - his brother Chritoolteram*
4. Which great organist did Bach walk 200 miles to hear? *Buxtehude*
5. What is a fugue? *A Musical Comp - first Melody continualy repeated*
6. What instrument did Bach give particular attention to at Cöthen? *Harp*
7. What position did Bach occupy in Leipzig? *Music director.*
8. What great affliction came to Bach in his old age? *Apoplexy.*
9. What is a Passion? *dealing with the last hours of Chris*
10. What else did Bach do besides composing? *An organ builder and a good music engraving.*

LESSON XIV.

HANDEL.

ALTHOUGH Bach and Handel were born in the same year, in German cities only a few miles apart, their life-work was very different. Bach was the greatest of all masters of polyphony. Handel was a master of polyphony, but he also wrote in monophonic forms—that is, with a melody accompanied by harmonies. This difference is due to the fact that the lives of the men differed greatly. Bach nearly always lived within a short distance of the city in which he was born, and his main work was along scholarly and religious lines. Handel, however, traveled widely and interested himself in dramatic music as well as in religious music. Handel's works have always been more popular than those of Bach, and he was greater than any musician of his day except Bach.

Georg Friedrich Handel was born at Halle in 1685. His family name was originally Händel, which would make the correct German pronunciation Hayn'-del, but this was changed to Handel when he went to England. Handel's father was a surgeon, who wanted his son to become a lawyer, but his talent for music was so great that many friends of the elder Handel persuaded him to let the boy study with an able organist named **Zachau** (tsah-cow). At the age of eleven he played the clavichord, organ, violin and *Oboe,* a wind instrument, so well that he was taken to Berlin as a prodigy. At twelve his father died and he was brought up by his

75

mother, who was a minister's daughter.   At seventeen he became organist of the Cathedral at Halle and entered the University in that city.   One year later he became a member of an orchestra in Hamburg, playing second violin for the purpose of getting wider experience.   The next year he produced four operas.   At the same time his organ playing was attracting much attention, and like Bach he paid a visit to Buxtehude, the great organist, at Lübeck.   In 1740 he also produced his first passion oratorio.

His restless spirit, however, soon led him to travel in Italy, where he remained for three years, from 1707 to 1710.   Here he was received everywhere by musicians with great enthusiasm.   He wrote much in Italy, including two operas, *Rodrigo* (ro-dree'-go) and *Agrippina* (agrip-pee'-na), and two oratorios in Italian style.   In 1710 he became choirmaster to the Elector of Hanover, but shortly thereafter went to London, where his operas *Rinaldo* (ree-nal-do) and *Teseo* (teh-seh-o) were very successful.   In England he wrote some church music to English words—the *Utrecht Te Deum* and *Jubilate* (ju-bih-láh-te)—for a public celebration.   This won him the disfavor of his patron, the Elector of Hanover, who later became the king of England, as George I.   Handel regained the royal favor by writing some music—the *Water Music*—for a water festival held on the river Thames, which pleased the king immensely.   From this time (1715) to his death (1759) Handel received salaries from the British court.

In 1720, when Handel was thirty-five years old, he produced his first English oratorio, *Esther*.   In the same year a stock company was organized to give opera at the Royal Academy of Music (London).   Handel and the Italian composer Bononcini were directors.   Handel wrote fourteen operas for

Georg Friedrich Handel.

this company, but during the next year the rivalry between
Handel and Bononcini became so keen that the political parties

THE BLIND HANDEL BEING LED TO THE ORGAN.

of the day took sides in the fight, and this resulted in riots
in the theatre, which brought ruin to the undertaking. Handel
then organized a company of his own with a view to saving

HANDEL AND KING GEORGE I. OF ENGLAND.

When George I. was Elector of Hanover he permitted Handel, who was his court musician, to visit England on leave of absence. Handel failed to return to Hanover at the end of this period, and when George became King of England, Handel naturally lost the royal favor. This was only regained after Handel had written music for a Water Festival, held on the river Thames. This music pleased the King immensely.

THE BOY HANDEL PRACTISING IN THE GARRET.

The story runs that Handel's father forbade his boy to have anything to do with music. A friendly apothecary, noticing

his reputation. For this he wrote thirteen operas. Again his rival, Bononcini, attacked him by forming a rival company. Competition was so sharp that both companies failed. Handel, as a result, lost all he had saved, and besides had a slight stroke of paralysis.

He again turned his attention to oratorio and wrote the works by which he is now best known—all of which were written after the age of fifty-three. His most famous oratorios are *Saul* (1739), *Israel in Egypt* (1739), *The Messiah* (1742), *Samson* (1743), *Judas Maccabæus* (mak'-a-beus) (1747), *Joshua* (1748), *Solomon* (1749), *Theodora* (the-o-do'-ra) (1750), and his last work, *Jephtha* (1752). Although all of these works are given occasionally, the most famous is *The Messiah*, an oratorio upon Christ's life, which was first produced in 1742 in Dublin, Ireland, while Handel was on a concert tour. This work has probably been given publicly more times and in more countries than any other musical work for large chorus.

Handel became almost totally blind six years before his death, but continued his work until a few days before his end, in 1759. He was buried in Westminster Abbey (London). He was a naturalized Englishman and his works made an impression upon English music that has lasted for a century and a half. Personally, he was blunt but jovial. He had many enemies and also many staunch friends. Owing to his great industry and genius he earned much money. He wrote with great rapidity. "The Messiah" (a book of about 180 pages) was written in twenty-eight days. Handel never married.

The last public appearance of this great master was at Covent Garden, the famous London musical centre, on April

6, 1759. Upon this occasion he directed a performance of his famous oratorio, *The Messiah.* This was only eight days before his death. Blindness did not interfere in the least with his performance at the organ and during his last years he was idolized by the public. As an indication of the astonishing fondness for Handel which has always existed in England we may note that a festival given in London, in 1784, to commemorate the one hundredth anniversary of the birth of the famous composer (1685) brought the promoters of the festival thirty-five thousand dollars profit, a truly prodigious sum in those days.

TEN TEST QUESTIONS.

1. What are the main differences between the works of Bach and Handel? *Bworte Polyphony — Handel wrote monophonia*

2. When and where was Handel born? *Halle 1685*

3. In what occupation was Handel's father engaged? *Surgeon*

4. Tell something of Handel's wonderful talent in his youth.

5. What leading instruments did Handel play? *Clavicord, Organ Ob*

6. Tell how Handel lost the favor of the Elector of Hanover and how he won it back.

7. Tell of Handel's work as a composer of operas in London.

8. How old was Handel when he commenced to write his great oratorios? *35*

9. Which is considered Handel's greatest oratorio? *The Messia*

10. What great affliction came to Handel in old age? *Blindness*

LESSON XV.

FRANZ JOSEPH HAYDN AND THE DEVELOP-
MENT OF THE SONATA AND
THE SYMPHONY.

WE HAVE already had something to say about the sonata, but to understand the sonata thoroughly you must take up the study of musical form. Strictly speaking, the word sonata means a single piece or movement, but it is now used to signify a set of three or more, the *first* one of which is generally the sonata.

A sonata is based upon two themes, called the principal and secondary themes. Each theme is given twice, the principal theme both times in the principal key; the secondary theme is first given in the key a fifth above the principal key, called the dominant key; when repeated it is given in the principal key. If the sonata is in a minor key, the secondary theme is given the first time in the relative major key. What are called subsidiary themes are often added, generally after the secondary theme.

The first movement is generally in rapid tempo. The second movement is generally in slow tempo, and is usually one of the rondo forms. The final movement is in rapid tempo, either in rondo form or sonata form.

The first printed sonata is said to have been written by **Johann Kuhnau** (koo'-now), died 1722. Kuhnau wrote many sonatas which were much admired. The sons of the great composer, Johann Sebastian Bach, namely, **Wilhelm**

Friedmann Bach, Johann Christian Bach, and especially Carl Philip Emanuel Bach, did much to develop the sonata.

This classical form, however, did not reach its height until it had been treated by **Haydn** (high'-dn), **Mozart** (mo'-tsart) and **Beethoven** (bay'-to-ven). The first of these, **Joseph Haydn**, was born in Rohrau (ro'-row), Austria, in 1732. His father was a wheelwright. The talent of the boy was

HAYDN'S BIRTHPLACE.

discovered early and at the age of six he went to study with a relative, J. M. Frankh (frahnk). At eight he joined the famous choir at St. Stephen's Cathedral, in Vienna, where he stayed for over nine years, studying and singing. Here he obtained free support and free instruction in singing. At the age of seventeen he was dismissed from the choir, and had it not been for friends he might have starved. He practiced on the clavichord, the violin and at musical composition, his model for sonata writing being the works of C. P. E. Bach.

FRANZ JOSEPH HAYDN.

During the next six years he wrote his first mass, a comic opera (music since lost) and his first quartet for four stringed instruments. For a time he studied under the famous teacher Porpora, serving as his valet in payment. He had a few pupils and played now and then for pay, and in this way he obtained money to purchase theoretical works. These he studied thoroughly and worked with unceasing pains to improve himself.

His ability soon became known and he secured wealthy patrons who provided him with means to continue his work. One of these, Count Morzin of Bohemia, had a fine orchestra, and while conducting this in 1759 Haydn wrote his first symphony. A *Symphony* is a work for orchestra constructed along lines similar to those of the sonata.

Two years later Haydn became assistant-choirmaster at the country-seat of Prince Paul Esterhazy (es'-ter-hah-zy), in Hungary. In 1766, after Prince Michael Esterhazy had succeeded his brother, Haydn was made conductor of one of the finest private orchestras in the world. His surroundings were of the most inspiring, notwithstanding the fact that his position was that of a servant in the prince's home. Haydn remained in the Esterhazy palace for nearly forty years, and while there wrote many of his most important works.

The prince died in 1790, and Haydn went to London to conduct some concerts. There he was received with enormous enthusiasm, and Oxford University conferred the degree of Musical Doctor upon him. He returned to Vienna, but went back to London in 1794, meeting with even greater success. There he heard the oratorio music of Handel, and later he wrote his famous oratorios, *The Creation* and *The Seasons*. When the French entered Vienna in 1809 Haydn is said to

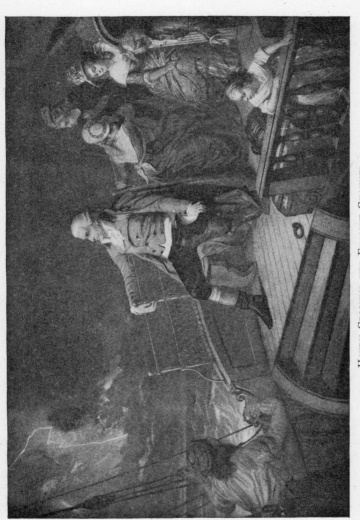

HAYDN CROSSING THE ENGLISH CHANNEL.

When Haydn returned from his first trip to England a terrific storm arose, which was said to have made a remarkable impression upon him and influenced several of his later compositions.

have died of excitement and old age during a bombardment of the Austrian capital. He is buried in Vienna. His instrumental works number nearly seven hundred, including one hundred and twenty-five symphonies and fifty sonatas and pieces for piano. His vocal works include his oratorios, thirteen operas, fourteen masses (Haydn was a devout Catholic), thirty motets, including the famous *Seven Last Words from the Cross,* which is frequently given to this day.

Haydn's music is considered bright and happy, and his disposition was charming and sunny, notwithstanding the fact that forty years of his life were spent with an irritable, disagreeable, trouble-making wife of low birth. Musicians in Haydn's time thought so much of him that he was called "Papa Haydn."

TEN TEST QUESTIONS.

1. Give a description of a sonata. *It is based upon two the*
2. Who wrote the first sonata ever published? *Johann Kuhna*
3. Who was the first of the three great masters to bring the sonata to its highest form? *Haydn*
4. In what famous church did Haydn sing as a boy? *St Stephens Called*
5. When did Haydn write his first symphony? *1759*
6. Who was Haydn's famous patron? *Count Morgin of Bohemia*
7. Tell something of Haydn's visit to England.
8. Tell something of Haydn's death. *excitement old*
9. What did the musicians of Haydn's time call him? *Papa Haydn*
10. Tell something of Haydn's works.

LESSON XVI.

WOLFGANG AMADEUS MOZART.

ALTHOUGH Haydn is given great credit for his splendid work as a writer of sonatas and symphonies, he had a pupil who was born twenty-three years later, in 1756, at Salzburg (sahlts'-boorg), Austria, and who died in 1791, eighteen years before the death of Haydn, who was such a genius that he influenced Haydn to make many changes and improvements in his own works. This remarkable composer was **Wolfgang Amadeus Mozart** (mo'-tsart), one of the greatest masters of all time and a genius of the highest class. At three he picked out little melodies at the keyboard; at four he could play little pieces, and at five he could compose creditably. At six he could play somewhat difficult violin music at sight, and played in public, while at seven he could play the organ; and at the age of ten Mozart was without doubt the greatest of all prodigies, for he could play the clavier, the violin and the organ with the skill of a master. He had also written by this time a symphony, two Italian arias (elaborate vocal solos), pianoforte sonatas and one part of an oratorio. At twelve he had written an opera and a comic opera, and when he reached fourteen he had written a grand opera and some fugues.

This marvelous boy was the son of the musician and composer **Leopold Mozart,** who took the greatest possible interest in his son's training. At the age of four, when most children nowadays are just starting in kindergarten, Mozart and his sister **Maria Anna** (aged five) received their first lessons from their father. Two years later the elder Mozart took his children to Vienna to play before musical critics and also

MOZART'S BIRTHPLACE IN THE AUSTRIAN CITY OF SALZBURG.

Mozart is still the great hero of Salzburg. The above house is preserved as a museum, and the monuments and the theatre show the devotion of the citizens of Salzburg to Mozart. Every few years Mozart festivals are given, at which great artists appear.

before the Emperor of Austria. This was the first of a series of ten long trips or tours made by Mozart, so that before he was twenty-five years of age he had visited many of the

Wolfgang Amadeus Mozart.

great cities of Germany, France, Austria, England, Switzerland and Italy.

The father arranged these trips for three purposes:

1. To broaden the views of his wonderful child, by making him acquainted with the ways in which the different people of Europe lived and thought.

2. To make his great talent known to the nobility of Europe, so that he might obtain a post as choirmaster or director at some royal palace.

3. To enable him to meet the great musicians of his time, and to profit by knowing them.

In this way he met the great Haydn, and learned much from him, but so remarkable was Mozart as a child and youth that he was looked upon everywhere as a great master. Thus, when he was twenty-one he was thought by many musicians to be equal to any living composer. His first important opera, *Idomeneo* (e-do-meh-neh'-o), was produced in Munich in 1781. Mozart was then twenty-five, and thereafter he wrote four others, which have lived through one hundred years; and when they are produced in great opera houses to-day they seem as bright and fresh and beautiful as they did to those who heard them a century ago. These operas are: *The Departure from the Seraglio* (say-rahl'-yo), *The Marriage of Figaro* (fee'-gah-ro), *Don Giovanni* (jo-van'-nee) and *The Magic Flute.*

Mozart's works, as a whole, include many songs, fifteen masses, several choral compositions for the church service, seventeen sonatas for piano (two-hand) and five for piano duet (four-hand), several *Concertos* (kon-tsher'-tos) and other pieces for the piano (a concerto is an instrumental solo in sonata form, accompanied by orchestra or band of instruments), twenty-six quartets in sonata form for four-stringed instruments, almost twenty operas, and forty-nine symphonies and other works for the orchestra.

Notwithstanding this great number of works, Mozart spent money so freely that his income was wasted, and his wife, Constanza Weber Mozart, whom he married in 1782, suffered much. Mozart's disposition was free and easy. He was a great wit, but was unfortunately influenced by many bad friends. He never secured a royal post that brought him large returns, although he held two posts in noble courts. Owing to his easy habits he was a pauper when he died in 1791 and was buried in the cemetery given over to the city paupers. One of his last works was a *Requiem* (reh'-kwe-em), the Catholic Church service in memory of the dead, which he was engaged to write. While working upon it he told his friends that he knew he was working upon his own requiem. Aside from his spendthrift habits, his character is described as being very generous, lovable and beautiful. As a child and youth we learn that he was considered most handsome. His skill as a performer was greatly admired by all musicians of his day, while the greatest masters of the art during the past century were almost of one mind in believing that no man has ever lived who wrote more beautiful melodies than Mozart.

TEN TEST QUESTIONS.

1. What influence did Mozart have on Haydn?
2. When and where was Mozart born?
3. Was Mozart's father musical?
4. Tell something of Mozart's remarkable sister.
5. How old was Mozart when he wrote a grand opera?
6. How many countries did Mozart visit as a youth?
7. Name four famous operas of Mozart.
8. Tell something of Mozart's other works.
9. Tell something of Mozart's wasteful habits and unfortunate poverty.
10. What was Mozart's last work?

CHRISTOPH WILLIBALD GLUCK.

LESSON XVII.

CHRISTOPH WILLIBALD GLUCK AND THE REFORM OF THE OPERA.

WE HAVE already seen how much attention was given to the opera in the seventeenth century, not only in Italy, but in Germany, Austria, France and in England. We will now study the life of a man who did more to improve the opera than any of those who went before him. This man was **Christoph Willibald Gluck** (glook), who was born in Nüremburg in 1714. He was the son of a game-keeper; that is, a man who looks after the wild animals in a district set apart by a nobleman for his private hunting. When he was twelve years old he was sent to a Catholic school, where he was taught clavier, organ, violin and 'cello. Later he gave music lessons and played at country dances to support himself, until the wealthy Count Melzi (melt'-zee) took him to Milan, Italy, where he studied under a noted teacher, **Sammartini** (sam-mahr-tee'-nee). He produced his first opera in Milan when he was twenty-seven years of age.

During the next twenty-one years he traveled much and wrote many operas which were exceedingly successful at the time, because they were written in the style of the operas which were popular in that day. Among these were *La Semiramide* (seh-mee-rah'-mee-deh) and *Telemacco* (teh-leh-mahk'-ko), but Gluck was convinced that he could write in a much better style, and also that the musical fashions of the day were not of the best. Therefore, in 1762, he wrote an

95

opera called *Orfeo* (or-feh'-o) *ed Euridice* (yu-ree'-dee-cheh), which contained so many new ideas and changes that the public was at first much astonished. His next opera was *Alceste* (1767), in which he made still more startling changes, but this work did not meet with special favor with the public. Then he wrote *Paride ed Elena* (pa-ree'-deh ed eleh'-na), 1770, and by this time the critics were becoming accustomed to his new ideas and took a liking to them.

In 1774 he produced a new opera called *Iphigenie en Aulide* (if-ee-jeh-nee on o-leed) in Paris. Had it not been that Marie Antoinette, then Queen of France, had been a pupil of Gluck in Vienna, the jealousy of the composer's enemies would have made it impossible for him to produce the work. As it was, however, the opera was an immense success, and many of Gluck's other works were produced in Paris.

In the year of the outbreak of our Revolutionary War (1776) an operatic war started in Paris, which is equally famous in musical history. Gluck's enemies, headed by the composer Piccinni, fought in every possible way to end his new methods and bring back old ideas. Gluck was fighting for musical liberty; Piccinni, for slavery to old-fashioned customs and dying musical laws. In 1778 both wrote the music to a *Libretto* (lee-bret'-to) called *Iphigenie en Tauride* (if-ee-zheh-nee ong taw-reed), but Piccinni's was not completed until 1781. Gluck's opera was so great that musicians everywhere recognized it as a masterpiece. After Gluck's death, which occurred in Vienna in 1787, Piccinni showed his appreciation of his rival by trying to collect money for a memorial concert to Gluck.

Gluck was very determined and was always a hard student. He was somewhat vain and lacked generosity. His later years were one long fight to make his ideas known to the world. His main purpose was to make music assist the *Action,* or the expression of the story of the play, rather than simply having a string of songs with connecting speeches set to music and called *Recitatives* (ray-see-ta-teef'), with little real musical bearing upon the play itself. Gluck wrote thirty operas, and seven of these influenced most of the opera writers who followed him. In 1754 the Pope made him Chevalier (shev-al'-e-eh) of the Golden Spur, and he is sometimes called Chevalier Gluck. Although Gluck wrote little but operatic music, the music is so important that he is ranked by German critics among the six great classical masters: Bach, Handel, Haydn, Mozart, Gluck and Beethoven. The last-named we shall study in our next lesson.

TEN TEST QUESTIONS.

1. What composer did the most to improve operatic conditions in the seventeenth century?

2. How did Gluck support himself while a student?

3. How old was Gluck when his first opera was produced?

4. Why did Gluck decide to change his style, although his operas had already met with success?

5. Were the operas written in Gluck's later style successful at first?

6. Which famous queen assisted Gluck?

7. When did the opera war between Gluck and Piccinni start?

8. What was Gluck's main purpose in reforming the opera?

9. Name three famous operas by Gluck.

10. Whom do the Germans call the "six great classical masters"?

7

Ludwig van Beethoven.

LESSON XVIII.

LUDWIG VAN BEETHOVEN.

WE HAVE learned how Haydn and his pupil Mozart developed the sonata and the *Symphony,* and now we shall learn of the great master who brought these two artistic musical forms to their highest stage. This was **Ludwig van Beethoven** (lood'-vig fan bay'-to-ven), who was born in Bonn, a little German city on the river Rhine, in 1770. His grandfather was a fine musician who came from Belgium to Bonn as *Kapellmeister* (kap-pel'-my-ster) or *Choirmaster,* in 1733. Beethoven's father, who was a professional singer, was a drunkard and ofttimes a very cruel man. Beethoven's mother was a cook and had, it is said, a very sweet disposition. Had it not been for her, the boy would have suffered greatly from the father's harsh severity. The parents were very poor, and the father's sole interest in his son was to make money out of him. He forced him to practice so hard that the little Beethoven soon hated practice, although he loved music. Like Mozart, Beethoven could play at a very early age (four), and when he was thirteen he was already a composer and a conductor (or player on the *Cembal*) (tshem-bal) at the theatre. A year later he commenced to earn his first money as assistant court organist to his teacher, Neefe.

When Beethoven was seventeen, he went to Vienna, where Mozart heard him and said: "He will make a noise in the world." Later he was instructed by the violinist **Ries** (rees) and played *Viola* (ve-o'-la) in the theatre orchestra. Twice

BIRTHPLACE OF LUDWIG VAN BEETHOVEN IN THE GERMAN CITY OF BONN, ON
THE BANKS OF THE RIVER RHINE.

Beethoven met Haydn while the latter passed through Bonn, and thereafter at Vienna, in 1792, where somewhat later he studied counterpoint with Haydn for two years.   In addition to this, Beethoven studied for one year with a famous teacher named **Albrechtsberger** (ahl'-brechts-berger).

He was a very earnest student and formed the habit of keeping note-books in which to jot down his ideas.   These ideas he worked over and over with untiring patience, and many think that this was one of the habits which led to his greatness.

Although he was ill-bred, low-born and often very blunt in his manners, he had many powerful and noble friends, who overlooked his independent ways in their admiration for his unquestioned genius.   As a pianist he was admitted to be without a rival, for he was also a great musician, and that meant that everything he played he understood.   This enabled him to give every measure of the music the right artistic expression.   So great was his ability and force as a man that, although before Beethoven's time the musician was often placed on the same plane as the servant in a royal house, Beethoven was never looked upon in this way, although he was assisted by giving instruction to wealthy noblemen.   In this way and through government pensions and royalties on his compositions he secured his living.

Beethoven's last years were made miserable by his incurable deafness, which came on him about 1800, and by the disgraceful life of his brother's son, of whom Beethoven was guardian.   Beethoven died in 1827, of dropsy, resulting from a cold.   His death occurred during a frightful thunderstorm.

Beethoven wrote in practically all the musical forms.   His greatest works are his symphonies, in which he introduced

BURR — AND DALLLING FOR THE FORTUNE

so many new and grand ideas that they have not been excelled, although nearly a century has passed since they were written. Haydn wrote one hundred and twenty-five symphonies, Mozart forty-nine, but Beethoven only nine. These nine, however, were the fruit of years of work and endless collection and development of musical ideas. Although all the symphonies are great, the most famous ones are the third or *Eroica* (ay-ro'-e-ka), written in honor of the great French soldier-emperor Napoleon; the fifth, the sixth or *Pastoral,* and the ninth or *Choral* symphony (in which there is a great choral setting of a poem by the German poet Schiller) and which took five years of hard work to compose. Beethoven wrote twelve beautiful *Overtures,* and many of them are now played almost as frequently as the great symphonies. His one opera is *Fidelio,* and although occasionally produced, it is not thought to be as great as his symphonies. He wrote an oratorio, *The Mount of Olives,* two masses and several smaller works for orchestra and chorus. He wrote over two hundred and fifty songs, only a few of which are sung now. His pieces for the piano include thirty-two sonatas for two hands and one for four hands, and one hundred other pieces in smaller forms. He wrote nine sonatas for violin and five for *Violoncello* (chel'-lo). His concertos include five for piano and one for violin. Some of his most beautiful music was written for combinations of four (*Quartet*), five (*Quintet*), six (*Sextet*), seven (*Septet*), and eight (*Octet*) insruments of the string and wind varieties.

Beethoven's music as a whole is so grand, so firmly founded upon sound musical laws, so full of great musical skill, so full of power and strength and yet so beautiful, that no master of any time can be declared greater.

Beethoven in his latter years became bad tempered and sour, always looking upon the black side of things. This was due very largely to his illness and to his great disappointment in the behavior of his nephew Carl. Nevertheless, the Viennese public had such a respect for the genius of Beethoven that he was looked upon as one of the greatest men of the country. When he died, his funeral was attended by a multitude of people of all classes, and the services were almost as elaborate as those given to kings and emperors.

TEN TEST QUESTIONS.

1. When and where was Beethoven born? *Born 1733 -*
2. Tell something of Beethoven's grandfather and of his father and mother. *His father was a drunkard and his mother a cook, father a very cruel man. If it was not for his ma he would not lived*
3. How old was Beethoven when he commenced to study? *When he cou*
4. What did Mozart say of Beethoven when Beethoven was a young man? *He will make a noise in the world.*
5. With which famous teachers did Beethoven study? *Haydn*
6. Tell something of Beethoven's habit of keeping note-books. *of down*
7. Tell something of Beethoven's personality. *ill formed - low born -*
8. What great affliction came to Beethoven in later life? *deafness*
9. How many symphonies did Beethoven write? *9 —*
10. Tell something of Beethoven's other works. *, He wrote over*

250 songs. 32 Sonata

LESSON XIX.

FRANZ SCHUBERT.

THE works of Beethoven were so great that they made the way of the composers who followed him somewhat hard. Beethoven's ideals were so high and he was such a hard worker that to equal him seemed an impossibility. Nevertheless, many writers feel that if **Franz Schubert** (frahnts schoo′-bayrt) had had equal opportunities and had not died at the very early age of thirty-one, he might have produced works which in number and importance would have equalled those of Beethoven. Schubert was born in 1797, when Beethoven was twenty-seven years old, and died in 1828, just one year after the death of Beethoven. Schubert was the son of a schoolmaster in the village of Lichtenthal (lic′-ten-tahl), near Vienna, and received his first musical instruction from his father and his elder brothers. They were very poor, but the little boy received instruction from the choirmaster Holzer, and at eleven he sang in the parish choir. His voice was so beautiful, however, that he was placed in the emperor's choir, and he remained in the choir school until he was sixteen. He was first a member of the school orchestra, then first violin, and later, much to his delight, he was allowed to conduct now and then. Here, also, he heard much fine music and some operas.

At this time his musical gods were Beethoven and Mozart; so when he left the choir school in 1813 and taught elementary subjects in his father's school, in order to escape being forced to go into the army, he commenced to compose

Franz Schubert.

with great rapidity. The remainder of his life was a struggle for existence, made miserable by his irregular, unbusiness-like habits, his timidity and modesty and his fondness for jovial companions who led him into loose methods of living. He had many friends, and among them was the well-known Viennese baritone, **J. M. Vogel** (fo-gel), who recognized Schubert's genius and who did everything in his power to help him. No doubt the friendship for Vogel, as well as the acquaintanceship with the poet Mayrhofer (meyr'-ho-fer), led Schubert to write many of his wonderfully beautiful songs. Schubert taught at different times in the home of Count Johann Esterhazy (es'-ter-hah-zy), and in 1822 he met both Beethoven and Von Weber, the operatic composer, of whom we shall learn more later. Had Schubert been a pushing, business-like man, he could have used these influential friends to assist him to secure a larger income, but he shrank from anything of this kind, and even when he was offered the position of court organist his shyness and hatred for anything that would require him to be in a certain place at a certain time each day led him to let this fine opportunity pass. In 1827 Schubert met Beethoven. The latter was amazed to learn of the number and wonderful beauty of Schubert's works. One year later a public concert of Schubert's works was given for the first time. This was favorably received and Schubert made some money from it, but ill-health and mental worry soon led to his death. All he owned at this time was worth only about $20, but his father and his brothers carried out his earnest request to be buried beside Beethoven.

Most of his later life was passed in miserable surroundings and in great poverty, although his affectionate nature brought

SCHUBERT COMPOSING THE MUSIC FOR HIS FAMOUS SONG CYCLE, "THE MILLER SONGS."

him many friends. He was very fond of poetry, and read constantly when he was not composing. He wrote some six hundred and fifty songs, which are considered models of their class. His symphonies number ten, some of them incomplete. He wrote fifteen dramatic works, but was not particularly successful in this style, except in the case of his overtures, one of which, *Rosamunde,* is still popular. He wrote twenty-one piano sonatas and three duet sonatas and a great number of smaller pieces for the piano. He wrote much for chorus, including two sacred cantatas (one of which, *Miriam's Song of Victory,* is well known), six masses and several motets and part-songs of a non-sacred kind.

Schubert's works are filled with beautiful melodic ideas, but his early training is considered weak and faulty by many writers. He apparently composed without difficulty, the melodies coming as fast as he could write them down. His most famous work is probably the *Unfinished Symphony* in B minor. In his songs he followed the idea of the poet very closely, and such songs as *The Erl King; Hark, Hark, the Lark; Serenade, Ave Maria, The Wanderer* and the sets known as *The Winter Journey* and the *Miller Songs* should be heard by all music students.

TEN TEST QUESTIONS.

1. When and where was Schubert born?
2. Tell something of Schubert's youth.
3. What did Schubert do immediately after leaving the choir school?
4. What characteristics made Schubert's life a struggle?
5. What turned Schubert's attention to song writing?
6. Tell something of Schubert's last days.
7. How many songs did Schubert write?
8. Tell something of his other compositions.
9. Name some of Schubert's most famous songs.
10. Which symphony is considered Schubert's greatest work?

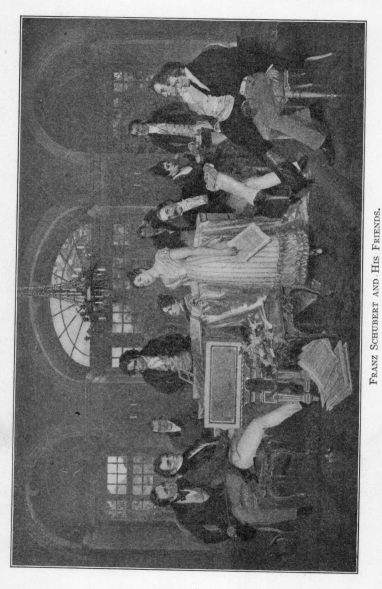

FRANZ SCHUBERT AND HIS FRIENDS.

Schubert was very convivial and had many friends. Some of his greatest songs were written for the amusement of his circle of friends.

LESSON XX.

CARL MARIA VON WEBER, AND HIS OPERATIC REFORM.

WE HAVE seen how the operatic works of Monteverde and Gluck were so original in many ways that they set an example for all composers who followed them. We now come to **Carl Maria von Weber** (vay-ber), a composer who also made great improvements in the opera and who is the last of the very great masters who lived at the same time with Beethoven, about whom we shall study. Von Weber was born at Eutin, near Lübeck, Germany, in 1786. His father was the choirmaster and band leader of the village and was the uncle of Constanz Weber, whom Mozart married. Thus von Weber and Mozart were cousins by marriage. The Weber family was very musical, and some half-brothers of Carl had been pupils of Haydn.

Carl's mother was an actress and a singer, and the elder Weber, during the first twenty-five years of his son Carl's life, moved from town to town with his talented family, giving concerts and plays. In this way they traversed most of Germany, and young Weber was really brought up in the theatre.

When Carl was ten he studied piano with Heuschkel (hoysh-kel), and to this teacher much of Weber's excellent knowledge of the piano is due. Two years later he studied composition under Haydn's brother, **Michael Haydn,** at Salzburg, and the next year he took up the study of organ under Court Organist Kalcher (kal'-cher) at Munich.   His first opera, *The Woodmaiden,* was written when Weber was only fourteen.   During the following two years he wrote another, called *Peter Schmoll.*   He then moved to Vienna, and his acquaintance with the musicians Vogler, Haydn, Beethoven and **Hummel** (hoom'-ml) inspired him to attempt to make better and higher aims.   He accordingly began a course of self-study that brought excellent results.

At eighteen we find him conductor of the theatre at Breslau, and three years later he became secretary to the Duke of Würtemburg (veart'-tem-boorg), who was both a weak and a bad man.   Weber fell a victim to the loose life of the court, and incurring the king's disfavor he was, fortunately for himself, banished, and went to Mannheim, where he overcame his bad habits.   During the next ten years he rose rapidly in ability as a composer, and his fame as a performer led to his appearance in many German cities.   For a time he held a post as director of the Prague (prayg; in German pronounced prahg) Theatre, but his masterly work led to a call from the beautiful city of Dresden, where, by an enormous amount of labor and attention to details, he made the court operatic performances exceedingly fine.   Here he wrote the first of the operas upon which his future fame was to rest— *Der Freischuetz* (dare fry-sheetz).   His health failed him and he gave up his post to travel.   Later, he was persuaded to move to Vienna, where two other notable operas, *Euryanthe* (oy-ree-an'-te) and *Oberon* (o'-be-ron), were written.   In 1826 he went to London to conduct some performances, and died there, of consumption, the same year.

Personally, Weber was very charming, very broad in his views and very magnetic.   He is most celebrated for his

8   CARL MARIA VON WEBER.

operas, in which he introduced many new ideas. He caught the German love for the mysterious and fairy-like old legends, and set music to plays upon these subjects in such a way that much of the stiffness which marked operas before his time was lost. In this he laid the foundation for the magnificent work of Richard Wagner, who called his operas music-dramas or music-plays. Weber also wrote much very fine music for the piano, including four piano sonatas, eight sets of piano variations, two piano concertos and a piece known as *Concertstück* (concert piece), which has been played a very great deal, as has his ever-popular *Invitation to the Dance,* His works for orchestra and for chorus include two symphonies, several overtures, two masses and some fine works for male chorus.

TEN TEST QUESTIONS.

1. When and where was von Weber born?
2. How was von Weber related to Mozart?
3. Tell something of Weber's youth.
4. Why was Weber's position as secretary to the Duke of Würtemburg an unfortunate one?
5. In what city did von Weber achieve great distinction as an operatic composer?
6. Name three celebrated operas by von Weber.
7. In what way did Weber's operas differ from those of other composers who came before him?
8. Which great composer was influenced by the works of Weber?
9. Was Weber's work confined to operatic composition?
10. Name some of Weber's works for piano and orchestra.

LESSON XXI.

FELIX MENDELSSOHN-BARTHOLDY.

Von Weber, as we have learned, developed the romantic opera and Beethoven had found out that the strict laws set down for musical composition were by no means always good ones. Beethoven found methods of producing beautiful music by means not based entirely upon these laws, and other musicians of his time felt that Beethoven was right. Thus, much of Beethoven's music is called romantic. The word classical was reserved for music that followed more strictly the laws of models used by Bach, Handel, Scarlatti, Haydn and Mozart, while the music of the freer style was called *Romantic*. Thus, all music that is difficult is by no means "classical," and because music is of the romantic style is no reason why it should be thought less important than classical music. The word "classic" really means a model believed by good judges to be the best of its kind. Thus, many of the works of Bach, Haydn, etc., were considered models, and those who did not follow the strict models were called "romanticists."

In **Felix Mendelssohn-Bartholdy** (men'-dels-sohn-bar-tol'-dy) we find a composer who could write equally well in the classical and in the romantic styles. Mendelssohn was born in 1809 at Hamburg, Germany. His grandfather, Moses Mendelssohn, was a noted Jewish philosopher, and his father was a wealthy banker who had become a Christian. His mother's name was Bartholdy, and Mendelssohn adopted this to distinguish him from the other members of the family. Mendelssohn's sister **Fanny** was also a remarkably talented musician.   Everything possible was done to give the children

PENCIL DRAWING OF MENDELSSOHN AS A BOY.

the best in musical, general and social training.   Like Mozart and Beethoven, Mendelssohn's talent was very marked at an early age, for by the time he was ten years old he played in

Felix Mendelssohn-Bartholdy.

public, and at twelve he composed in a remarkable manner. He had the advantage of lessons and advice from such excellent teachers as Berger (bair'-ger), Zelter (tsel'-ter) and Henning, in Berlin, and Mme. Bigot (bee'-goh) and **Cherubini** (ker-roo-bee'-nee), in Paris.   Later he studied with the renowned pianist **Moscheles** (mosh'-eh-les).   He knew most of the great musicians of his day.   When he was only seventeen he was able to write an overture to Shakespeare's play, *A Midsummer Night's Dream,* which is now thought to be the most perfect and beautiful musical work of art ever produced by any one at that early age.   His first and only real opera, *The Marriage of Camacho* (ka-ma'-cho), was performed in Berlin in 1827.   It was liked by the public, but owing to the unfairness of the theatre director, **Spontini** (spon-tee'-nee), who disliked Mendelssohn, the opera was withdrawn.

Mendelssohn was very fond of the works of Bach and Beethoven, and in 1828 he succeeded in giving Bach's oratorio, called *The Passion of St. Matthew,* which had had its first performance one hundred years previously in Leipzig (Germany).   This led to a greatly increased interest in Bach, which has lasted to this day.   In 1829 Mendelssohn began making a series of tours which, during the next few years, took him to England, Scotland, Italy and Austria, and which not only gave him wider views, but greatly quickened his desire to compose. He was a most excellent pianist and a fine conductor, and everywhere he was greeted with great popular enthusiasm. He was a man of great personal charm, and aside from his ability as a musician he could draw sketches with much artistic skill and was a most fascinating letter writer.

He conducted some important festivals in 1833 and in 1835.

For a time he was located as town musician at Düsseldorf.
His greatest work, however, was done at Leipzig, where in
1835 he became conductor of a very famous orchestra, known
as the "Gewandhaus (gay-vahnd'-house) Orchestra," and
which is still one of the great orchestras of the world.   Here
all the musical conditions were in his favor and he accomplished
much excellent work.

After many trips to other German cities and to England,
where his oratorio *St. Paul* was produced in 1837, Mendelssohn was called to Berlin in 1840, where he was given the
post of kapellmeister (musical director) to the courts of
Saxony and Prussia.   He desired, however, to found a music
school, and the conditions not being right in Berlin, he went
back to Leipzig in 1843, and there founded the Leipzig Conservatory, which has become one of the most famous of all
music schools.

Mendelssohn was very popular as the leader of great music
festivals, and in 1846 he conducted many, including one at
Birmingham, England, where his oratorio *Elijah* was first
given.   He was greatly admired in England, and he made
a greater impression upon English music than any other
musician, with the possible exception of Handel.   In 1847 he
made his last trip to England; upon his return he learned of
the death of his much-beloved sister, and he never recovered
from the shock.   He died the following year and thousands
of music-lovers throughout the world mourned his loss.   He
was a high-minded, lovable man, with noble purposes and very
great ability.   In 1837 he married the daughter of a Swiss
Protestant clergyman and five children were born to them.

Of his famous works we may name his four symphonies,
seven overtures of great charm, both in melody and in skill in

writing for the orchestra; two piano concertos, one violin concerto, music for different combinations of stringed instruments,
many exceedingly beautiful piano compositions, including the
Songs without Words; six organ sonatas; organ preludes and
fugues; music for plays of the noted writers Goethe (gayt'-
eh), Sophocles (sof'-o-klez), Racine (rah-seen') and Shakespeare, the famous oratorios *St. Paul* and *Elijah,* and some
very celebrated musical settings of the Psalms.

We cannot pass by Mendelssohn without mentioning some
of his famous friends, who either lived and worked at the
same time or who were connected with the great school which
Mendelssohn founded. Other more famous musicians of Mendelssohn's day will be studied in complete chapters. In attend-
ing concerts and in reading books on music you will learn of
the following men, and it is interesting to know something
of their part in musical history:

Ludwig Spohr (spohr), born in Brunswick, Germany, in
1784, died in 1859, was a remarkable violinist and a very able
composer. He had the advantage of knowing such musicians
as Beethoven, Rossini (ros-see'-nee), Paganini (pah-gah-nee'-
nee), the great violin virtuoso, Weber and Mendelssohn, and
was one of the first to realize the greatness of Richard Wagner.
Spohr, like Mendelssohn, was very popular as a conductor of
large music festivals, both in Germany and in England. For
thirty-five years he was court choirmaster at Cassel. He wrote
over two hundred works, including nine symphonies, ten
operas, eight overtures, fifteen violin concertos, a noted violin
method and four oratorios, of which *The Last Judgment* is the
best known.

Niels W. Gade (gah'-deh), born in Copenhagen, Denmark,
in 1817; died in 1890. When very young he became a violin

virtuoso. In 1843 he went to Leipzig, Germany, where for five years he enjoyed the friendship of Mendelssohn and Schumann. His cantatas, his eight symphonies, five overtures and four violin sonatas, as well as his fascinating piano pieces, are highly regarded, although their resemblance to Mendelssohn and Schumann is marked at times.

William Sterndale Bennett, born in 1816 at Sheffield, England, died in 1875, was a graduate of the Royal Academy in London and became famous as a pianist and a composer, even before he went to Leipzig in 1842 and became a friend of Mendelssohn. His compositions, which include a symphony, an oratorio, four overtures and many pianoforte works, are striking and skilful, but lack the kind of harmonies which, musicians claim, add warmth and *Tone-color* to a composition.

Ferdinand Hiller, born in Frankfurt in 1811, died in 1885, like Mendelssohn, came of wealthy Jewish parents. He was a conductor and a composer of wide renown in his day, and his compositions, which include six operas, three symphonies, four overtures, two oratorios, three piano concertos and many fine works for the piano, are original, strong and interesting, but are now performed very rarely.

Moritz Hauptmann (howpt'-man), born in Dresden in 1792, died in 1868, was at first a violinist with many noble admirers and patrons, and later a composer and a theorist. He is now known principally for his very able work as the teacher of counterpoint and composition in the early days of the Leipzig Conservatory, where his original ideas and deep learning impressed many of the famous students who came under him. Hauptmann was a pupil of Ludwig Spohr.

Julius Rietz (reets), born at Berlin in 1812; died in 1877. He was a life-long associate of Mendelssohn and taught com-

KARL REINECKE.

Reinecke was one of the greatest teachers of our time. Many foremost musicians of to-day were among his pupils.

position at the Conservatory of Leipzig. Aside from being a virtuoso on the violoncello, he wrote many deserving compositions, including three symphonies and four operas.

Karl Reinecke (rye'-neck-eh), born at Altona, Germany, in 1824; died in 1910. He became a virtuoso pianist at a very early age and showed a great fondness for the works of Mozart. He became a friend of Schumann and of Mendelssohn and later was court pianist at Copenhagen. After many tours he finally went to Leipzig, and as the conductor of the Gewandhaus Orchestra, as a teacher in the conservatory, and, later, as director of the same institution he won world-wide fame. His works number over two hundred and fifty, and include three symphonies, nine overtures, six operas and operettas, an oratorio, two masses and a host of interesting pieces.

TEN TEST QUESTIONS.

1. State the principal difference between *classical* music and *romantic* music.
2. Is classical music more important than romantic music?
3. When and where was Mendelssohn born?
4. Tell something of his ancestry.
5. What advantages did Mendelssohn have in youth?
6. What great art-work did Mendelssohn write when he was seventeen?
7. Tell something of the revival of Bach's *St. Matthew Passion.*
8. Tell something of the *Gewandhaus* orchestra, and the founding of the Leipzig Conservatory.
9. Was Mendelssohn popular in England?
10. Tell something about each of the following musicians who were friends of Mendelssohn: Spohr, Gade, Bennett, Hiller, Hauptmann, Rietz, Reinecke.

ROBERT SCHUMANN.

LESSON XXII.

ROBERT SCHUMANN, AND THE AGE OF MUSICAL ROMANCE.

OF ALL the famous friends of Mendelssohn, the most celebrated was **Robert Schumann** (shoo-mahn), and although he was directly connected with the Leipzig Conservatory, under Mendelssohn, we have reserved an entire lesson for him, because many writers feel that he was the greatest and most original composer of his time and because it was necessary for you to understand the difference between the romantic and the clasiscal in music in order to understand Schumann's position.

Schumann was born in 1810 at Zwickau (tsvik'-ow), and although neither of his parents was musical, they were cultured and educated people, his father being an author, translator and bookseller. He showed talent for music in his seventh year, and at twelve he learned to play the piano creditably and had tried his hand at composition. He was very fond of reading, particularly the romantic writer "Jean Paul" Richter. His imagination was said to be very remarkable and as a youth he was a "dreamer." When his father died, Schumann was only sixteen, and his mother determined to make a lawyer of him. With this in view, he went to Leipzig, where he also studied piano under the excellent teacher, Friedrich Wieck (veek). Then he went to Heidelberg (hide'-el-bayrg) University, and then to Italy, but his mind was ever far more upon music than upon law.

Finally, he obtained his mother's permission to become a musician and went to Leipzig again to study under Wieck, with a view to becoming a virtuoso or concert pianist. He used a device to make his fourth finger work more freely and strained his hand so much that he was compelled to give up

ROBERT AND CLARA SCHUMANN.

all thought of a career as a pianist. He next gave his attention to musical composition and studied under Heinrich Dorn.

In 1831 he learned of the works of a new pianist in Paris, and his admiration for him led him to write an enthusiastic article about him. This pianist-composer was the great Chopin (sho'-pang). After that, Schumann wrote many articles which made many friends for him, and among them were several enthusiasts whom he formed into a group, which he called the *Davidsbund*. Later, in 1834, he founded the famous musical newspaper called the "Neue Zeitschrift für Musik" (The New Journal for Music), and remained its editor for ten years.

In 1836 he fell in love with Clara Wieck, the daughter of his teacher, who was then only seventeen, but who had already become famous as a pianist. Her father opposed the marriage with such severity that Schumann was obliged to go to law to get his consent. Their married life was ideal, and his wife inspired him to write some of the most famous of his many works.

When Mendelssohn organized the Leipzig Conservatory, Schumann taught composition and piano in the institution, but he has never been considered a great teacher or a great conductor. He was too retiring and too original. He made several lengthy and successful tours with his wife, who played his compositions to perfection. He was a very hard worker and suffered much from overwork. In 1844 he moved to Dresden, where he became acquainted with Wagner and Hiller and later directed a male chorus. In 1850 he went to Düsseldorf, on the river Rhine, to direct a male chorus. Overwork brought on insanity, and in 1854 he attempted to commit suicide by jumping into the Rhine, but was rescued by boatmen. He was taken to a private asylum near Beethoven's birthplace, Bonn, and died in 1856.

Schumann composed in almost every style, but he is best known for his very original and beautiful piano pieces, his four symphonies, his dramatic music for his opera, *Genoveva* (**geh**-no-veh′-vah), and for *Faust* (fowst) and *Manfred,* his cantatas and his two hundred and fifty songs, many of which represent the highest excellence in the art of song-writing.

Schumann's pianoforte pieces are so different from those written by his predecessors that he may be said to have founded a style of his own, that is quite as distinctive as that of the wonderful Polish-French musician Chopin. Some famous critics regard the symphonies of Schumann as the greatest works in this form that have appeared since Beethoven.

TEN TEST QUESTIONS.

1. When and where was Schumann born? *1810 - Zwickau*
2. What profession did Schumann's mother desire to have him adopt?
3. Who was Schumann's famous piano teacher? *Friedrich Wieck*
4. Why was Schumann obliged to give up his career as a pianist? *strained*
5. Tell something of Schumann's work as a critic and as a writer.
6. Tell something of Schumann's famous wife. *She played better than*
7. Was Schumann a successful teacher and conductor? *not very*
8. What terrible affliction came to Schumann late in life? *Insane*
9. How many songs did Schumann write?
10. Name some of his other famous works.

LESSON XXIII.

SOME FAMOUS OPERA WRITERS OF THE NINETEENTH CENTURY.

OF THE opera writers of the nineteenth century, the ones whose works are most frequently performed are Wagner and **Verdi** (vair'-dee). We will devote more attention to these writers later, and at present consider some who, although not so famous, may still deserve to be studied by the earnest student.

Of the Italians, the most famous is **Gioachino Rossini** (ros-see'-nee), who was born in 1792, at Pisaro, Italy, and died in 1868. His musical talent became evident at a very early age, and at fifteen he entered the Conservatory at Bologna (bo-lo'-nya) and studied counterpoint. He became particularly fond of Haydn and Mozart, and his school companions made fun of him for his German taste. His first opera was produced in Venice when he was eighteen years old. His success as an opera writer was very great and he visited many European capitals, but in 1824 he went to Paris, where his greatest work was accomplished as director of the Théâtre Italien. Of his forty operas, three, *The Barber of Seville, Semiramide* (seh-mee-rah'-mee-deh), and *William Tell,* are well known to-day, as are his religious works, *Stabat Mater* (stah-bat mah'-ter) and *Messe Solennelle.* Rossini's music is bright, skilful and vigorous, although not very profound.

9 129

After Rossini, the two Italian composers of the time who were most popular were Bellini and Donizetti.

Vincenzo Bellini (bell-le'-nee) was born at Catania (ca-ta'-nia), Italy, in 1810, and died in 1835. His father, an organist, was his first teacher. At eighteen he studied under the best masters in Naples and became familiar with the German as well as the Italian writers of the day. His best-known operas to-day are *La Sonnambula* (sonn'-am-bu-la), *Norma* and *I Puritani* (ee poor-ee-tahn'-ee), and his melodies are noted for their simple charm and beauty.

Gaetano Donizetti (doh-nee-tset'-tee) was born at Bergamo, Italy, in 1797, and died in 1848. His early education included music, and while he was a soldier at Venice he wrote his first three operas. At first he was not very successful with his works, but during his life he wrote sixty-five operas, including *The Elixir of Love, The Daughter of the Regiment, Don Pasquale* (pas-quall'-ee), *Lucia* (loo'-che-a) *de Lammermoor, Lucretia* (loo-krayd'-ze-a) *Borgia* (bor'-ja), which met with wide success and which are still produced. Donizetti's work is brilliant and taking, but lacks the deep and sincere character which marks great music.

Giacomo Meyerbeer (my'-er-bair), born in Berlin in 1791, died in 1864, was the child of well-to-do Jewish parents named "Beer." He adopted the Meyer to please a wealthy relative. As a child he was a concert pianist, but later became one of the most popular opera composers of his day, his most successful works being *Robert le Diable* (roh-bayr' lay dee-ah'-bel), *The Huguenots* (hoo'-geh-no), *The Prophet, Star of the North* and *L'Africaine* (laf'-re-kane). He was an able composer and had much real musical feeling, but was so anxious to secure popular favor that he cared more to

GASPARO SPONTINI.

GIACOMO MEYERBEER.

GIOACHINO ROSSINI.

GAETANO DONIZETTI.

VINCENZO BELLINI.

make his compositions showy than of real worth. Consequently, his work has been overshadowed by that of other composers.

The following is a list of other well-known opera composers whose works are less frequently performed to-day, but of whom music students and concert-goers may hear frequently:

ITALIAN COMPOSERS.

Luigi Cherubini (keh-roo-bee'-nee), born in Florence in 1760; died in 1842. Like Lully, Cherubini was born in Italy but is best known for the excellent work he did in the gay capital, Paris. His father was a cembalist (chem-ba'-list), and Cherubini received his first lessons from him. Later he went to study with **Sarti** (sar'-tee) in the Italian city of Bologna. When he was a young man he wrote some operas in the Italian style and was looked upon as an Italian composer, but in 1785 he went to Paris and remained there over fifty years. Here the great success of the composer Gluck led Cherubini to follow his style in some ways, and he produced several highly successful operas, the best known being *Les Deux Journees* (leh duh zhour-neh'), called in Germany *Der Wasserträger* (The Water Carrier). Cherubini was first teacher of composition at the Conservatoire and later director of the institution for nearly twenty years. He wrote, in all, fifty operas, and he is also famed for his excellent sacred works, which include eleven masses and two requiems, and are thought to be among the very finest music written for the Catholic Church service.

Gasparo Spontini (spon-tee'-nee), born in Ancona, Italy, in 1774, and died in 1851, was another Italian whose greatest fame was gained in other countries. He spent so much time in Germany and France that his Italian birth and early Italian accomplishments as a composer are sometimes forgotten. He went to Paris in 1803, where, eight years before, the great school of music, now known as the Paris Conservatoire, had been founded. This school added greatly to the interest in music in Paris, and Spontini found a fine field for his work. Here, as the director of the famous "Théâtre Italien" (Italian Theatre), he brought out Mozart's *Don Giovanni* and gave performances of Haydn's symphonies and other German music. Here he wrote and produced his famous operas, *Milton, Ferdinand Cortez, La Vestale* (ves'-tahl) and *Olympie*. The last-named is considered his greatest work, but recent revivals of *La Vestale* in Europe have been extremely successful.

In 1820 Spontini went to Berlin as director of the opera to the King of Prussia. Here he wrote three operas, including *Agnes von Hohenstaufen* (ho'-en-stow-fen), but the great success of von Weber and the fact that Spontini was a harsh, severe and disagreeable man led to the loss of his position and to an old age filled with failure and discomfort. Spontini's music deserves to be better known, since it is strong and full of character, although he had not mastered the art of composition, as had some of his famous rivals.

FRENCH COMPOSERS.

François Adrien Boieldieu (bwahl-dyay), born at Rouen, France, in 1775; died in 1834; best-known work, *La Dame Blanche*.

Daniel François Esprit Auber (o-behr), born at Caen, France, in 1782; died in 1871; director of the Paris Conservatory for nearly thirty years; best-known operas, *Masaniello* (massa-nee-el'-lo), *Fra Diavolo* (dee-a'-vo-lo), *Le Bal Masque* (mask) and *Manon Lescaut* (ma-non les'-ko).

Louis Joseph Ferdinand Herold (ay'-rold), born at Paris in 1791; died in 1833; best-known opera, *Zampa.*

A. E. M. Gretry (greh'-tree), born in Liège in 1741; died in 1813; best-known opera, *Richard Cœur de Lion* (kuhr-de-lee'-ong).

F. J. Gossec (gos-sek), born in Belgium in 1734; died in 1829; a noted violinist who wrote many symphonies and operas, his best-known work being *Les Pecheurs* (leh-peh-shers).

Fromantel Halèvy (ah-leh'-vee), born at Paris in 1791; died in 1862; he was of Jewish descent and was a pupil of Cherubini at the Conservatory; best-known work, *La Juive* (The Jewess).

German Composers.

Gustav Albert Lortzing (lort'-zing), born in Berlin in 1801; died in 1851; best-known works, *Czar und Zimmerman, Undine* and *Der Waffenschmied* (vaffen-schmeet). These works are still very popular in Germany.

Johann Strauss, Jr., born in Vienna in 1825; died in 1899; son of Johann Strauss, a famous Viennese writer of dance music; best-known works, *Die Fledermaus* (fleh'-dehr-mouse) and *The Gipsy Baron.*

Heinrich Marschner (marsch'-nehr), born at Zittau in 1795; died in 1861. *Der Vampyr* (vam-peer) and *Hans Heiling* are his best-known works. He was a really excellent composer, whose works, though mostly difficult, should be better known.

F. von Flotow.

Daniel Auber.

Johann Strauss, Jr.

Michael Balfe.

Albert Lortzing.

Unfortunately, many of the works of the composers we have discussed in this chapter have suffered from having weak and uninteresting librettos or books. No matter how fascinating the music, it is difficult, in these days, to keep audiences interested in stage performances that are so out of keeping with common sense and which have so little appeal to the imagination. For this reason many of these composers are now limited to the concert stage, and since the majority of their works were written to accompany acting, and are unsuited to performance without costume, scenery, action, etc., many of their compositions are gradually sinking into disuse.

TEN TEST QUESTIONS.

1. Of what great German composers was Rossini fond? *Haydn & M*
2. Name two of Rossini's most famous operas. *The Barber of Seville, will*
3. What are the best-known operas of Bellini? *La Sonnambula, Norma & ...*
4. Tell something about the work of Gaetano Donizetti. *He wrote while a sol...*
5. Why is it that Meyerbeer does not hold so high a position as Wagner or Weber? *his work was over shadowed —*
6. Tell something of the work of Cherubini as a composer and as an educator. *50 operas — 11 masses & requiems.*
7. In what great cities did Spontini do most of his work? *Paris —*
8. Name six famous French composers of operas and give the titles to their works. *Boieldieu — Auber — Herold, Gastry — Gosrec — Halevy.*
9. Name three popular German opera composers and give the titles of their works. *Lortzing — Strauss Jr — Marschner —*
10. Are any of the works of the foregoing composers performed in this day? *yes —*

LESSON XXIV.

GREAT TEACHERS AND WRITERS OF MUSIC USED IN PIANO STUDY.

QUITE as important as the great composers are the musicians who have been their teachers, and we will now study the lives of some whose principal work was musical education, particularly those who taught piano. This is necessary because it leads to a better understanding of the men who influenced many of the great composers, and because the compositions and names of these teachers frequently come before the student.

We shall learn, later, that the great composers Chopin, Schumann, **Brahms** (brahmz) and **Liszt** (list) introduced so many extreme methods of playing the piano that they practically revolutionized the art. The teachers whose names follow represent the era of Clementi and Beethoven, which in itself was one of quite as much importance for the art of pianoforte playing as that of Liszt and Chopin. Clementi's style was so original that his compositions were thought very novel in their day.

Muzio Clementi (moot'-si-o cleh-men'-tee), born at Rome, 1752, died in 1832, was at first an organist and a composer of church music. At the age of fourteen he went to London and amazed his audiences by his wonderful playing. Thereafter he made many famous tours throughout Europe, and composed over one hundred sonatas in the classical style, which, it is said, Beethoven used as models for some of his first works. Clementi's best-known educational work was a series of technical studies known as *Gradus ad Parnassum*. In later life he went into the business of making pianos and displayed much ability as a business man.

Johannes Ladislaus Dussek (doo'-scheek), born in Czaslau, Bohemia, 1761, died in 1812, commenced his studies at the age of five with teachers in Catholic schools. At the age of twenty-two he studied with Emanuel Bach in Hamburg. He made many extensive tours as a *Concert-pianist* and wrote fifteen concertos, fifteen sonatas and many pieces of educational value for the pianoforte, as well as a piano method. His compositions are original and often brilliant.

John Baptiste Cramer (krah-mer), born at Mannheim, 1751; died in 1858. Cramer was educated in London, where he studied with Clementi. He was successful as a concert-pianist and as a teacher. He knew both Haydn and Beethoven, and the latter praised his playing very highly. He wrote one hundred sonatas, seven concertos, many studies and a piano method. He founded a publishing house in London in 1828. His studies are not used as much as formerly, but they are valuable as preparatory exercises for the works of the composers who wrote before the time of Chopin and Liszt. Liszt, although representing a new style, used them and recommended them highly.

Johann Nepomuk Hummel (hoom'-ml), born in Presburg, Hungary, in 1778, died in 1837, was a pupil of Mozart, at the age of seven. Later he studied with Albrechtsberger and **Salieri** (sal-yeh'-ree). He knew Beethoven well, and his remarkable experience made him much sought as a teacher, and he had many famous pupils. He was an able performer,

JOHANNES L. DUSSEK.   JOHN FIELD.
CARL CZERNY.   MUZIO CLEMENTI.   J. B. CRAMER.
    ADOLF HENSELT.   STEPHEN HELLER.

but his playing was thought somewhat "stiff and hard." He wrote four operas, much church music and many sonatas, concertos and pieces for piano. He also wrote a lengthy piano method.

John Field, born in Dublin, Ireland, in 1782, died in 1837, was a wonderful child-performer and was employed by Clementi to show off pianos in Clementi's store in return for instruction. Aside from tours on the continent, he spent most of his life in London and in Russia, where he was very popular. He wrote seven concertos, many sonatas and many *Nocturnes* (noc'-toorns), which were the forerunners of the great nocturnes written by Chopin. A nocturne is a short piano-piece in song form, and the word means "a piece to be played in the evening or night." Field was a pianist of high rank and as a teacher he was exceptionally successful.

Friedrich Kalkbrenner (kalk'-bren-ner), born in Paris, 1788, died in 1870, was a pupil of Clementi and Albrechtsberger. He was an exceedingly fine pianist and his keyboard technique was considered very remarkable. After tours in Germany and France, he settled in Paris as a teacher and was unusually successful. He once offered to teach Chopin, but the offer was spurned. Artistically, Chopin was already much greater. Kalkbrenner wrote some sonatas and many very fine studies for piano; but, lacking the artistic value of the Chopin studies, and the technical value of those of other writers, they are little used now. He also wrote a pianoforte method.

Carl Czerny (tschair-nee), born in Vienna, 1791, died in 1857, was a pupil of his father and of Beethoven. He wrote over one thousand works in all forms of music composition. He is best known for his collections of studies for piano, particularly the *School of Velocity* and the *School of Legato* (leh-gah'-to) *and Staccato* (stac-cah'-to), which, together with volumes of selections from his works, have a world-wide use. His most famous pupils were Franz Liszt and **Theodore Leschetizky** (leh-shay-tit'-skee).

Ignaz Moscheles (mosh'-e-lehs), born in Bohemia, 1794, died in 1870, was a pupil of Dionys Weber, Salieri and Albrechtsberger. He also knew Beethoven well. He was a brilliant pianist and his success as a virtuoso was great in Germany, France and Holland. He resided in London over twenty years. In 1824 he taught Mendelssohn piano in Berlin, and when the latter founded the Leipzig Conservatory, Moscheles became the leading teacher of pianoforte in the institution. His concertos, sonatas and advanced studies, although not widely used, all show his thoroughness and mastery of the secrets of the piano.

Adolf Henselt (hen'-selt), born in Bavaria, 1814, died in 1889, was a pupil of Hummel. He was known as a pianist of the greatest finish and technical skill. For fifty years he was engaged in teaching at St. Petersburg. He was very modest and dreaded playing in public. He wrote a concerto and many shorter pieces. His piano studies, mostly very difficult, are among the finest pieces written for the student. Of these, *If I Were a Bird* is very popular.

Stephen Heller (hel'-ler), born in Hungary, 1815; died in 1888. At the age of seventeen, Heller was well known as a pianist in his own country. Like Henselt, he was very modest and sensitive and made few tours. In 1838 he went to Paris and remained there fifty years. He wrote many hundred beautiful short pieces, and his originality as well as his ability to create simple yet charming melodies, together with his knowledge of the art of pianoforte playing, make his works of the very first importance to the teacher and to the student.   The pupil who has not enjoyed the charm of Heller's best pieces and studies has missed much.

TEN TEST QUESTIONS.

1. What is the name of Clementi's famous series of studies?
2. Was Clementi a virtuoso?
3. Tell something of Dussek.
4. Where was Cramer educated?
5. What great masters did Hummel know?
6. What form did Field create which was much used by Chopin?
7. Which great composer did Kalkbrenner desire to teach?
8. Who was the teacher of Franz Liszt and Theodore Leschetizsky?
9. Who was the first leading teacher of pianoforte at the famous Leipzig Conservatory?
10. Which great pianist dreaded playing in public? Which great composer of simple études is particularly famed because of the originality and tunefulness of his work?

LESSON XXV.

FREDERIC CHOPIN.

WE HAVE already been obliged to refer to **Frederic Chopin** (sho-pang), the wonderful genius of the piano whose entrancingly beautiful works have made such an impression upon all musical art since his time. He was born near Warsaw, Russia, in 1809 (or, according to some authorities, 1810), and died in 1849. His father was a successful school teacher who, twenty-two years previously, had come from France and settled in Poland. His mother, a highly educated and cultured woman, was a Pole.

Parts of Poland had been seized by Russia, Austria and Prussia (1795), with a view to destroying the Polish nation. During Chopin's youth his mind was continually upon the unfortunate troubles of his country and upon the fruitless efforts of his countrymen to unite it. So powerful is the patriotic feeling of the Poles that even to-day, after a century has passed, the love of country in Poland is as strong as ever, and the Poles believe that the time will come when their nation will be restored to them. The loss of his country dwelt heavily on Chopin's mind and is said to have had the effect of making many of his compositions sad and sorrowful. His love of country is also shown in the strong and distinct characteristics of many of his pieces, particularly his *Mazurkas* (mah-tsoor′-kahs), which the great Polish pianist **Paderewski** (pah-der-eff′-skee) has declared to be his most interesting works. A mazurka is a Polish dance in three-four time.

Chopin's first teacher of music was **Zwyny**, a Bohemian, and so pronounced was the child's talent that he played a concerto in public at the age of nine. His general education was good, and at fourteen he entered the high school or "lyceum" and also became a pupil of **Elsner**, an excellent teacher, to whom Chopin always gave great credit. He commenced to compose dances and little pieces soon thereafter, so that when he was sixteen he published his first musical composition. His first public appearance as a pianist was

A PLASTER CAST OF THE HAND OF CHOPIN.

made in Vienna when he was twenty. During the next two years he played in German and Austrian cities, and finally settled in Paris, where he met and knew all of the famous musicians of the great "capital of art," as Paris was then called. Among these were Mendelssohn (then on a tour), Liszt, Meyerbeer, **Berlioz** (behr-lee-o), Bellini, Auber, Rossini, Cherubini and the conceited Kalkbrenner, who desired to teach Chopin.

Schumann was among the first to realize the great genius of Chopin and he published booklets praising Chopin's work,

FREDERIC CHOPIN.

which did much to make him famous. Chopin's bodily strength would not permit him to give extensive concert tours after he was thirty-six years of age. He made occasional trips to other countries and in 1837 went to England, but the number of his performances was limited.

About 1836-1837 he fell deeply in love with Mme. Dudevant, who had become famous as a novelist under the name of "George Sand." Chopin's nature was tender, affectionate and almost woman-like. Mme. Dudevant was a woman of great intellectual power and was at times coarse and mannish. Her influence over Chopin was not of the best, although he believed that she was the source of his inspiration.

When he was about thirty he was seized with consumption during a trip to the Island of Majorca. Notwithstanding this, he continued composing, and some of his greatest and strongest works were written when he was fighting to keep the flame of life in his body. He occasionally gave concerts, for which rarely more than one thousand tickets were issued, and these tickets were eagerly sought. After a trip to England and Scotland, he returned to Paris in 1849 and died of his dread disease. He was buried in Paris with much ceremony.

Chopin was a born aristocrat; that is, he preferred to move in what was thought to be the best society and disliked the so-called common or ordinary people. He had many whims, and was always dreamy and poetical. It is, perhaps, for this reason that his music is generally not so rugged and vigorous as that, for instance, of Beethoven and some other composers. Chopin was very fond of Bach, and although his own concert programs were usually made up exclusively of his own compositions, he practiced nothing but the works of Bach while preparing for his concerts.

He wrote almost entirely for the piano. His works include four ballades (extended piano pieces, said to have been inspired by old Polish legends), four *Scherzos* (skert'-zos), brilliant and lively pieces in three-four time (the word scherzo meaning "playful"); three piano sonatas, two concertos, fifty mazurkas, fifteen waltzes, several *Polonaises* (Polish national dances resembling the march, but in three-four time), nineteen nocturnes (short, poetic, song-like piano pieces; the word nocturne meaning "a piece to be played in the night"), twenty-five preludes, twenty-seven remarkable piano studies and other lesser-known pieces, as well as a few songs. So popular are Chopin's works that it is safe to say that one-third of the compositions found upon the programs of the great pianists who tour this country are by this famous master.

TEN TEST QUESTIONS.

1. Tell something of Chopin's birth and of his parents.
2. Tell something of the strong patriotism of the Poles.
3. Who were Chopin's first teachers?
4. In which great capital of Europe did Chopin make his home?
5. Who was the first great musician to spread Chopin's fame?
6. Was Chopin robust or delicate?
7. With what famous writer did Chopin fall violently in love?
8. What dread disease afflicted Chopin?
9. Why is Chopin's work as a whole not considered as rugged and vigorous as that of Beethoven?
10. Tell something of Chopin's works and of their popularity.

FRANZ LISZT.

LESSON XXVI.

FRANZ LISZT.

WE HAVE learned how the originality of Chopin led to many changes in pianoforte playing, and we shall now study about **Franz Liszt** (list), who by means of his marvelous technic so increased the scope of the instrument that the standards of playing were greatly changed. Liszt's wonderful velocity, his astonishing method of playing trills, runs, scales and octaves, together with the music he wrote, which inspired other performers to do likewise, upset all previous ideas of technic in piano playing.

Franz Liszt (born 1811, at Raiding, Hungary; died in 1886), was the son of a manager of the estates of the noble family of Esterhazy, which has contributed so much to musical history by their support of the great masters. The father was said to have been a fine amateur pianist, and when his son was nine years old he played so marvelously that a number of noblemen guaranteed his father one thousand dollars a year for six years, so that the wonderful child might continue his musical education. He was taken to Vienna and was placed under the famous teachers, Salieri and **Randhartinger** (rand-hart'-in-ger), and three years later astonished the Viennese public and won the enthusiastic praise of Beethoven.

He went to Paris, where he studied under **Reicha** (ry-khah) and **Paer** (pa-ehr), and produced an operetta called *Don Sancho* (san-ko) in 1825. During the next fifteen years he lived in Paris, teaching, composing and occasionally going upon successful concert tours. All the famous men and women interested in art, literature and music were his friends, and he became very intimate with Chopin, Paganini and Berlioz. Beginning with his twenty-eighth year, he started a series of concert tours which amazed all Europe and brought him considerable wealth. His generosity was magnificent. He helped hundreds who were in distress, and upon one occasion donated ten thousand dollars toward a monument to Beethoven, at Bonn. Some state that in his later years he played solely for charitable purposes, and it is well known that he gave his instruction without charge, since his private fortune permitted him to do this.

In 1849 he went to Weimar as court musical director. There he produced many notable operas at the opera house, when the composers of these works, Wagner, Berlioz, **Rubinstein** (roo'-bin-styne), **Cornelius** (kor-nay'-lee-oos) and others, had great difficulty in getting their new ideas accepted. Liszt's assistance was of enormous value to these composers. Owing to the failure of the public to appreciate Cornelius' opera, *The Barber of Bagdad,* Liszt left Weimar in 1850 for Rome. Here he became so much interested in religious work that he studied with a view to becoming a priest, and even won the title of "Abbe" or "Father." Ten years later he returned to Weimar, and the remainder of his life was spent in Rome, Weimar and in Budapest (where he became honorary president of the new National Academy of Music in the Hungarian capital) and at Bayreuth, where Liszt's friend, Richard Wagner, who had married Liszt's daughter, Cosima, had established his great opera house.

Liszt's works include three oratorios, three cantatas, eight symphonic poems, many masses and other orchestral works which indicate great ability in orchestral and choral writing. His piano compositions include an immense number of arrangements and transcriptions, ranging from the organ works of Bach and the orchestral works of Beethoven, Wagner, Rossini, Verdi, Berlioz, Mendelssohn, etc., to the most delicate songs of Schubert, Schumann, Arcadelt and others. He also wrote fourteen *Rhapsodies* (rap'-so-dees) or elaborate arrangements of Hungarian tunes, and a number of original pieces, studies, nocturnes, etc., which have great beauty and charm, but which are usually limited to the advanced player because of their extreme difficulty. His concertos, *Fantasias* (fan-ta-zee'-as) and other works with orchestra are played very frequently by great pianists. His songs are dramatic.

Associated with Liszt in his work were many friends and pupils, and we shall devote a little attention to three of these men before passing to Liszt's famous friend, Richard Wagner.

Joseph Joachim Raff (yo-a'-kim rahf), born in Laken, Lake of Zurich, in 1822, died in 1882, was almost entirely self-taught except for his fortunate association with famous musicians. His early life was one filled with hardshhips, owing to his irregular habits and lack of business ability. In 1850 he became assistant to Liszt at Weimar. Later he became a successful piano teacher, which led to the excellent position of director of the Dr. Hoch Conservatory at Frankfort-on-the-Main. He wrote over two hundred and thirty works, including two operas, eleven symphonies, nine overtures, a fine piano concerto and many very attractive and popular piano pieces. He was a skilful and talented composer, but was not above writing to suit the popular taste in times of need, although this was highly distasteful to him.

Peter Cornelius (kor-ney'-lee-oos), born in Mayence in 1824; died in 1874. He became associated with Liszt at Weimar, in 1852, but his opera, *The Barber of Bagdad,* failed in 1858, and he went to Vienna. Through Wagner's influence he secured a place in the Munich school of music, and in 1865 his opera, *The Cid* (thid), was produced at Weimar. Like Wagner, Cornelius wrote the texts or plays for his own operas, and he holds his position in musical history because his works were in parts so masterly that they cannot be forgotten, although he failed to win a place among the very greatest writers of his day; many of his songs are extremely beautiful and original.

Hans von Bülow (hants fon bee'-loo), born in Dresden, 1830, died in 1894, was a pupil of Schumann's famous teacher, Friedrich Wieck, and later of Franz Liszt, at Weimar. He was a remarkable virtuoso and became court pianist at Berlin in 1858. His memory was phenomenal and he was said to have had an almost unbelievable number of pieces at his fingers' ends. In 1867 he became royal musical director and director of the Conservatory at Munich. He visited America in 1875 and in 1885. As a director and an editor of musical works, as well as a pianist and teacher, his work for the cause of musical education was of unquestioned importance. He championed the cause of Wagner and did much to make that composer's works popular.

Karl Tausig (tow'-sig), born in Warsaw, 1841, died in 1871, was one of Liszt's most remarkable pupils. Liszt himself declared that Tausig excelled him in some technical points. He founded a school for advanced pianists in Berlin and wrote a technical method which has been the foundation for many later and more improved works of the same kind.

In a later chapter we shall mention the work of some twenty more pupils of Liszt who have attained high positions in the musical world. Those who knew Liszt personally were invariably intense admirers of both the man and his works. In later years his compositions, particularly his symphonic poems, have been regarded with the highest esteem by composers of foremost rank, and this form has been employed by many modern masters. Lacking the formal limitations of the symphony and permitting the composer the freest field for his musical and poetical imagination the symphonic poem is more employed to-day than the older symphony form. The most discussed composer of our times, Richard Strauss, has written in this form with great success.

TEN TEST QUESTIONS.

1. How did Liszt's wonderful playing affect the musical compositions of the composers who followed him? *Made a Change*
2. Tell something of Liszt's remarkable ability as a child.
3. In what great cities did Liszt continue his musical education? *Vienna*
4. Was Liszt generous? *Yes.*
5. Tell something of Liszt's splendid work at Weimar. *He produced many operas*
6. Where did Liszt study with the view of becoming a priest? *Rome*
7. In what city did Liszt found a national music school? *Rome*
8. Give a short description of Liszt's work as a composer.
9. Tell something of the work of Raff and of Cornelius. *self taught man*
10. State something of the achievements of Von Bülow and of Tausig as pianists.

*Born in Dresden 1830 - 1894 —
pupil of Schumanns famous teacher —
Born in Warsaw 1841 - 1871 —
Liszts most remarkable pupil —*

RICHARD WAGNER.

LESSON XXVII.

RICHARD WAGNER AND "THE MUSIC OF THE FUTURE."

A GERMAN writer has recently made a list of the number of books written about the great composers. Those written about **Richard Wagner** (vahg'-ner) number over eight hundred, and this is nearly double the number written about any other composer. In this way you can see how important the works of this great master have been considered. So different was his music from that of those who went before him that it was called "the music of the future," which was a very truthful prophecy, because much of the music since the time of Wagner has been influenced by his remarkable work.

Wagner was born in Leipzig in 1813 and died in 1883. His father held a small position at the theatre, but died when Wagner was very young. His mother then married a poet, actor and artist named Ludwig Geyer, who took great interest in Wagner's training. The boy went to the Kreuzschule (kroits-shoo-leh) in Dresden and became wrapped up in his studies of German and Greek poetry, giving much attention to the drama or plays. At fourteen the family moved back to Leipzig and Wagner studied at the gymnasium and later at the university. In Leipzig he heard many orchestral concerts and determined to be a composer. His musical instruction was limited to a short period under **Müller** (meehl'-ler), **Altenburg** (al'-ten-boorg) and **Theodor Weinlig** (vine-lig). But he was one of those remarkable students who could see at a glance the foundation laws underlying the rules he desired to use. Consequently, he soon outstripped his teachers and made rules for himself. He studied the works of Beethoven with great care and wrote a symphony in classical style, which was played when he was twenty years old by the famous "Gewandhaus" orchestra. His first opera, *The Fairies,* was written in 1833 at Würzburg (vearts-boorg), where he was chorus director at the theatre, with a salary of ten dollars a month. The next year he went to Magdeburg as director for a theatrical company and wrote an opera called *Das Liebesverbot* (leebes-fehr-bote), which was produced in 1836, but was not particularly successful. His next post was as director at Königsberg (kay'-nigs-berg), where he married an actress, Minna Planer. The company at Königsberg failing, Wagner fled to Riga (ree'-ga), where he later became conductor and was enabled to map out his operas, *Rienzi* (ree-ent'-see) and *The Flying Dutchman.* In 1839 he left Riga for Paris, stopping at Boulogne to meet Meyerbeer, who Wagner hoped would assist him to get some work to do in connection with the opera. He was very unsuccessful, however, and every moment of his stay in Paris was a struggle for existence. He was obliged to do musical arranging of a lower order to get the necessities of life. The directors of the opera saw the dramatic value of his libretto of *The Flying Dutchman,* but laughed at his music. They secured the libretto and it was produced later, with music by Dietsch (deetsh), a French composer who is now practically unknown.

In 1842 Wagner left Paris for Dresden, where his operas *Rienzi* and *The Flying Dutchman* were produced with such great success that he was made court musical director in the following year. He wrote *Tannhäuser* (tan'-hoy-ser), 1845, and *Lohengrin* (lo'-en-green), 1847, and the newness of Wagner's ideas, as well as his peculiar method of orchestration or arranging his music for the instruments, together with his hasty temper and determination to have his own way in everything, brought him many enemies; and when he made political statements which were considered treasonable or against the Government he was obliged to flee to Liszt, at Weimar (1849). Liszt rushed him off to Paris, and from there Wagner went to Zurich, Switzerland. During the next twelve years he lived in exile from Germany, spending part of his time in Switzerland, part in France, part in Italy, part in Belgium and part in England. He was engaged upon many of the works which in future years were to be so tremendously successful; namely, *Das Rheingold* (rhine-gold), *Die Walküre* (dee val-kee-reh), *Siegfried* (seeg'-freed) and the glorious work, *Tristan and Isolde* (e-sol'-deh). In the year of the outbreak of our Civil War, *Tannhäuser* was given in Paris, but the opposition was so great that riots resulted from its performance. In 1861 permission to return to Germany was obtained, and he went to Vienna to assist in the production of *Lohengrin,* which, although written fourteen years previously, Wagner had never heard. He also attempted to give *Tristan and Isolde,* but after many rehearsals the performers declared the work so difficult that it was impossible, and Wagner, in despair, was obliged to give up. In these days the opera is frequently given in great opera houses.

In 1862 he made an extensive tour, conducting concerts in Germany, Austria, Hungary, Bohemia and Russia. He had planned many works of great importance, but was without the necessary money to provide for his needs while he was engaged in composing them. Shortly thereafter, **Ludwig II,**

known as "the insane king" of Bavaria, summoned Wagner
to his capital, Munich, and guaranteed him the support neces-

RICHARD WAGNER'S HOME AT BAYREUTH.

Wagner built this house according to his own plans and spent his latter years
here.   He is buried in the garden at the rear of this building, and beside him
were buried the bodies of his favorite dogs, at Wagner's request.

sary to carry out his ideas.   Here his *Tristan and Isolde* was
brought out in 1865.   Thereafter he finished *Die Meistersinger* (1867), which, although a great masterpiece, is his only

comic opera. *Siegfried* was completed in 1869. In 1871 he moved to the Bavarian city of Bayreuth (by-royt), where four years later, he completed the festival theatre built upon his original ideas, in which the orchestra is concealed from the view of the audience. In Bayreuth he completed the cycle or circle of four music dramas written about legends found in an old German poem known as the *Nibelungen Lied* (nee'-beh-loon-gen leed). This cycle includes the operas, *Die Götterdämmerung* (dee getter-day-meh-roongk), meaning "The Twilight of the Gods"; *Das Rheingold* ("The Rhine Gold"), *Die Walküre* and *Siegfried*. His last opera was *Parsifal* (par'-se-val), written partly around an old German legend of a religious character. Wagner died at Venice in 1883 and was buried in the garden of his home at Bayreuth. He was unquestionably one of the most powerful of all musicans and also one of the greatest of all dramatists. His character stands out in musical history as does that of no other composer. His powerful personality, his almost unbelievable capacity for work and his strong and original ideas produced works that have influenced most of the musicians who have followed him.

TEN TEST QUESTIONS.

1. By what term was Wagner's music called?
2. In what study was Wagner particularly interested while a boy in school?
3. How old was Wagner when his first symphony was played by the leading orchestra in Europe?
4. What was the name of Wagner's first opera?
5. Why was the opera *The Flying Dutchman* rejected at Paris?
6. Why was Wagner obliged to leave Dresden after his musical success as a conductor at the opera?
7. What works did Wagner write while in exile?
8. Why were the performances of *Tristan and Isolde* abandoned at Vienna?
9. Tell something of Wagner's wonderful work at Bayreuth.
10. Why is the *Nibelungen Cycle* so called?

LORENZO PEROSI.

GIACOMO PUCCINI.

GIUSEPPE VERDI.

GIOVANNI SGAMBATI.

RUGGIERO LEONCAVALLO.

PIETRO MASCAGNI.

LESSON XXVIII.

MODERN ITALIAN COMPOSERS.

In our early studies we learned of the tremendous influence of Italy in all musical work. At different times the musical excellence of the composers of other nations has outshone that of Italy. Italy has produced no symphonist equal to Beethoven, no piano composer equal to Chopin, nor any writer of music dramas equal to Richard Wagner, but during the latter part of the last century a number of composers arose in Italy whose works entitle them to permanent places among the masters. The most important of these was **Giuseppe Verdi** (vehr'-dee), who, although born in 1813 (the same year as Wagner), did not reach his greatest heights until 1871, when his famous opera *Aïda* (ah-ee'-dah) was produced. He was so talented that when he was ten years old he was the organist of Buseto, the village in which he was born. He studied in his native town and at Milan, where his first opera, *Oberto* (o-behr'-to), was produced in 1838, with great success, at the famous opera house known as La Scala (la skah-lah). A comic opera produced two years later was unsuccessful, and this, together with his grief over the death of his wife and two children, almost caused Verdi to abandon his musical career. The manager of the theatre, however, persuaded him to write two other operas, called *Nabucco* (nah-book'-ko) and *I Lombardi* (lom-bar'-dee), which were very successful. His next operas of note were called *Ernani* (air-nahn'-ee), *Atilla* and *Louisa Miller*.   He visited London and Paris and learned much from the observation of the styles of opera produced in these capitals.   His next works, produced between 1851 and 1867, were those by which he is now best known, although they are by no means his greatest operas.   They include *Rigoletto* (rig-o-let'-to), *Il Trovatore* (ill tro-vah-to'-reh), *La Traviata* (lah trah-vee-ah'-tah), *Un Ballo in Maschera* (mas-keh'-rah) and *Don Carlos*.   These operas brought Verdi's name to the very front rank of all Italian opera composers of his day, but, in the meantime, in Italy, Wagner's wonderful success was by no means escaping Verdi's attention.   He realized the value of Wagner's ideas and his broader view of the importance of the dramatic side or story of the opera.   Although Verdi was nearly sixty at this time, he commenced a series of operas that are unquestionably greater than his earlier works and which show the influence of Richard Wagner. The operas include *Aida* (ah-ee'-dah), *Falstaff* and *Otello*. *Falstaff* was written when Verdi was eighty years old.   Verdi wrote little except operatic music, but his *Requiem,* written in honor of a famous Italian statesman named Manzoni, is a work of great melodic beauty.   Verdi died in 1901 and his funeral was made a national event.   He was very warm-hearted and generous, and a magnificent home for aged musicans in Italy is one of his many charities.

A brief statement of the names and leading works of other Italian composers of recent years follows.   Most of these writers show the wonderful influence of Richard Wagner, but also indicate the Italian love for beautiful melodies and rich, warm harmonies.

Umberto Giordano (jee-or-dah'-no), born in 1867, has

written five operas, of which the best known is *Andrea Chenier* (an'-dre-a sheh-nee-eh).

Arrigo Boito (bo-ee'-to), born in 1842, has written four operas, the best-known work being *Mefistofele* (me-fis-to-feh'-leh). He also wrote the librettos for several of the best-known operas of Verdi.

Pietro Mascagni (mahs-kahn'-yee), born in 1863, has written several operas, of which the best known is *Cavalleria Rusticana* (cah-vah-leh-ree'-a rus-tee-cah'-nah).

Giacomo Puccini (poo-tschee'-nee), born in 1858, probably the greatest of present-day Italian opera writers, his most famous works being *La Boheme* (bo-ehm'), *Tosca* and *Madame Butterfly*.

Ruggiero Leoncavallo (lay-on-ka-vahl'-loh), born in 1858, has written over eight operas, of which the most famous is *I Pagliacci* (e pal-yatch'-ee).

Giovanni Sgambati (sgam-bah'-tee), born in 1843, a pupil of Liszt and a foremost pianist, composer and educator. Sgambatti was appointed director of the famous St. Cecilia Academy at Rome. He has written much excellent piano music, including a concerto for piano, as well as three symphonies of value.

Giuseppe Martucci (mahr-tootch'-ee), born in 1856; died in 1909. A modern composer of unquestioned merit, who has written an excellent piano concerto, a symphony and music in smaller forms along German lines.

Lorenzo Perosi (pay-roh'-see), born in 1872. An Italian priest and director of music at St. Peter's, in Rome, whose oratorios and music for the Catholic service have brought him fame.

Enrico Bossi (bos'-see), born in 1861, has written five

operas and some symphonic poems, but is best known for his music for the organ and for the church service. He is the foremost Italian organist of our time.

TEN TEST QUESTIONS.

1. Has Italy ever produced a symphony writer equal to Beethoven? *No*
2. When and where was Verdi born? *Italy – 1813 – 1871*
3. Name three or four of Verdi's better known but less important operas. *Aida. Otello – Rigoletto – Il Trovatore.*
4. How did Wagner's success affect Verdi's style? *Influence d' ...*
5. Name three of Verdi's greater operas. *Aida – Falstaff – Otello*
6. What famous charitable institution did Verdi found? *...home for...*
7. Name five other Italian opera composers and state which is the most famous. *Giordano – Boïto, Mascagni – Puccini*
8. Which famous Italian composer was a pupil of Franz Liszt? *Sgambati*
9. Which famous composer of the present day is director at St. Peter's?
10. Who is the foremost Italian organist? *Bossi –*

LESSON XXIX.

ANTON RUBINSTEIN.

OF ALL the many rivals of Franz Liszt, there is one who by his strong personality and wonderful ability stands supreme. Chopin could not be considered a rival of Liszt, since he did not try to execute the marvelous feats of technical skill that seemed mere trifles to Liszt. There was a pianist, however, whose technic and musical ability were so great that some who knew him and heard him considered him superior to Liszt as a performer, and some, indeed, think that he was a greater composer. This man was **Anton Rubinstein** (roo'-bin-styne), born in Wechwotynecz, Russia, 1830; died in 1894. He was a pupil of his mother and of the pianist, **Alexander Villoing**. When Rubinstein was ten, his teacher took him to Paris, where he played before Liszt and Chopin, who were both amazed at his talent. Later (1844), Rubinstein studied composition with **Dehn** in Berlin. After highly successful tours through many countries, he returned to St. Petersburg in 1848, and by the time this remarkable youth was twenty-three he had produced two operas on Russian subjects. Not satisfied with the local success of these works, he ventured forth again from Russia and created a sensation by his wonderful playing in Berlin, Paris and London. In 1858 he returned to St. Petersburg and was appointed court pianist and conductor of the court concerts. Four years later he founded the Imperial Conservatory of St. Petersburg and remained its director for five years. The next twenty years of his life were spent as a virtuoso, and his appearances were always events in the musical world.

In 1872 Rubinstein toured America and received forty thousand dollars for two hundred and fifteen concerts, which was considered an enormous amount in that day. Later, he refused one hundred and twenty-five thousand dollars to repeat the tour, as at the time he is said to have found musical conditions in America far from his liking. His technic, his deep musical feeling, as well as his marvelous memory, made his playing comparable only with that of Franz Liszt. In 1887, Rubinstein resumed the directorship of the St. Petersburg Conservatory for three years, and after this time he resided in Berlin and in Dresden, devoting his time mostly to composition. His great ambition was to be known as a composer and he wrote a very large number of compositions, including over thirteen operas, five concertos for piano, as well as many fine pianoforte pieces in smaller forms, including the *Melody in F,* which is among the most popular pieces ever written; six symphonies, of which the most famous is the *Ocean Symphony;* much excellent chamber music and some fine songs. Rubinstein was very jealous of the great success of Richard Wagner and frowned upon the latter's efforts. This was unfortunate, for it led people to compare Rubinstein's music with that of Wagner, whom Rubinstein never equaled in Wagner's own peculiar style, although Rubinstein wrote much music that entitles him to be ranked as a master. His music for pianoforte is marked by wide hand stretches in the form of chords and *Arpeggios* (ar-ped'-jee-os), which are unusual, since Rubinstein's own hand was singularly small for a virtuoso pianist. Before his death Rubinstein received the "Order of

ANTON RUBINSTEIN.

Vladimir," which made him a nobleman, and he also became an imperial councillor of the Russian state.

Rubinstein's brother, **Nicholas Rubinstein** (born in 1835, at Moscow; died in 1881), attained considerable fame as a teacher, and was declared by his brother Anton to be a better performer. This, however, was not the opinion of other judges. In 1864, Nicholas Rubinstein opened the now famous Moscow Conservatory, and while there taught many famous pupils, among whom was the virtuoso, **Emil Sauer.** He wrote several attractive pieces, but never devoted as much time to composition as his brother. Nicholas Rubinstein was a pupil of **Dehn,** in Berlin, and of **Kullak** (kool-lahk).

TEN TEST QUESTIONS.

1. Of which great pianist was Rubinstein considered the leading rival?
2. What did Liszt and Chopin think of Rubinstein's playing as a child?
3. When did Rubinstein found the St. Petersburg Conservatory?
4. When did Rubinstein make his tour of America?
5. Why did Rubinstein refuse to come back at the time?
6. What was Rubinstein's great ambition?
7. Of which great composer was Rubinstein jealous?
8. State one peculiar characteristic of Rubinstein's music.
9. Which is Rubinstein's most popular pianoforte composition?
10. Tell something of Rubinstein's brother Nicholas.

LESSON XXX.

GREAT FRENCH COMPOSERS OF THE NINE-TEENTH CENTURY.

IN THE foregoing lessons we have learned how important Paris had become as a centre of art and music. The very generous provisions made by the French Government in providing for a magnificent opera house and an efficient conservatory of music added wonderfully to the interest in music in that country.

In the early part of the century the most famous musicians of the great city seemed to be those who were born in other countries, such as Chopin, Liszt, Spontini, Cherubini, Meyerbeer and others. One French-born musician, however, after many terrible struggles, gained recognition for himself not only in France, but in other European cities. This musician was **Hector Berlioz** (behr'-lee-o), born at La Côte-Saint-André, France, 1803; died in 1869. His father was a doctor, who sent his son to Paris as a medical student, but Berlioz's interest in music led him to study the flute and the guitar. Later he studied at the Conservatory, in the meantime earning his living by singing in a theatre chorus. Although failing five times, he finally wrote a cantata, called *Sardanapale* (sar-dah-nah-pah'-leh), which won the "Prize of Rome" (Prix de Rome, pronounced pree deh rome). This is a prize the French Government awards to the best students at the Conservatory, which entitles them to three years' travel and life abroad, most of which is spent at a building in Rome devoted solely to this purpose. Berlioz, however, was restless and returned to Paris after an absence of less than two years. Here he wrote many compositions and also became one of the leading critics of the city. It was only after an extensive tour of other European cities, where he was received with great enthusiasm, that the Parisian public really appreciated his work. He was an able conductor, and his work upon orchestration was of great importance. He found new ways of using the orchestral instruments and greatly increased their effectiveness in many ways. He also was devoted to what is called *Program Music;* that is, music which attempts to depict some series of events, such as a story or a legend. His most famous works are his dramatic legend, *La Damnation de Faust,* the opera *Les Troyens* (leh troy-ong), the religious works, *Te Deum* and *Messe des Mortes,* and his remarkable symphonic poems called *Harold in Italy, Benvenuto Cellini* (ben-veh-noo'-to cheh-lee'-nee) and *Romeo and Juliet.* Berlioz died in 1869.

Berlioz, by his originality and by the number of his works, stands alone among French composers of the last century, but many other masters whose works are now frequently performed deserve more attention than the limits of our history will allow us to give. They are all unquestioned masters, but their styles differ very widely.

Charles Gounod (goo'-no), born in Paris, France, 1818, died in 1893, was first taught by his mother, who made many sacrifices to secure an education for her son. After graduating from the Paris Conservatory he turned his attention to sacred music. His first operas were not received with much favor; consequently, when he wrote his famous opera, *Faust,* some time passed before it was produced in 1859. The opera

CAMILLE SAINT-SAËNS.
HECTOR BERLIOZ.   CHARLES GOUNOD.
JULES MASSENET.

AMBROISE THOMAS.
CLAUDE A. DEBUSSY.
GEORGES BIZET.

was wonderfully successful and has been produced hundreds of times since in all the great cities of the civilized world. Another opera of wide renown is his *Romeo and Juliet.* He also wrote an oratorio called *The Redemption,* which has been frequently performed, as has his highly successful cantata, *Gallia.* His sacred songs are very extensively used. Gounod's works are filled with melodies which are often very beautiful and which remain long in the memory. His works lack great strength, and they cannot be classed with the operas of Wagner or the later operas of Verdi.

Georges Bizet (bee-zay), born in Paris, France, 1838, died in 1875, was one of the most original and talented of all French composers. His handling of his fascinating opera *Carmen* has won the most enthusiastic admiration of all musicians. He wrote other operas and orchestral music as well as piano pieces, but was evidently just coming to the realization of his wonderful powers when death cut short his work, at the early age of thirty-six. Musicians often express the belief that had Bizet lived he would have become the greatest of French musicians. *Carmen* is a monument in itself.

Ambroise Thomas (am-bro-az to-mah), born in Metz, 1811, died in 1896, is best known through his operas, *Mignon* (meen-yong), *Hamlet* and *Francesca di Rimini* (fran-ches'-ka dee ree'-mee-nee), although he wrote in all over twenty-five operas and ballets. He was a graduate of the Paris Conservatory, and in 1871, upon the death of Auber, he became head of the institution and in this position did much to further the cause of musical education in France. His works also include two masses and two cantatas and some chamber music. Thomas was exceedingly skilful in his treatment of the orchestra and produced many novel effects. Few masters were so familiar with the musical needs of the stage, and had Thomas' purpose been deeper, his position might have been with that of Wagner, Weber and Gluck.

Cesar-Auguste Franck (frahnk), born at Liege, Belgium, 1822, died in 1890, was a pupil of the Liege Conservatory and of the Paris Conservatory, in which institution he later became professor of organ. His best-known work is a symphonic poem with chorus, called *Les Beatitudes*. Franck was a very original thinker and a very thorough worker. It is thought that his boldness in trying to get out of old-fashioned ruts in harmony and melody has had a great influence upon the leading French composers of the present day.

Camille Saint-Saëns (sangt-sah-ong), born at Paris, 1835, (still living, 1910), is a most brilliant and able composer who has written in many styles. The most popular of his ten operas is *Samson and Dalila,* which has recently been revived in Europe and in America with great success. He has also written four symphonic poems of decided charm, five symphonies, five piano concertos and much excellent music for piano in smaller forms. Saint-Saëns is a fine pianist, and a recent concert tour in America, made in his seventieth year, was extremely successful. He is also a fine organist.

Jules Massenet (mas-seh-neh), born at Monteaux, 1842 (still living), one of the most brilliant and gifted of the French composers of our time. He is a graduate of the Paris Conservatory, and besides taking the first prize in piano playing and fugue writing, he also took the "Prix de Rome." He has written much for the orchestra, but his fame rests upon his operas, of which the most famous are *Le Roi de Lahore* (roa de la-hore), *Le Cid* (le thid), *Werther, Thais* (tah-is), *Manon, La Navaraise, Le Jongleur de Notre Dame.*

Achille-Claude Debussy (deh-bus'-see), born at Paris, 1862, (still living) ; studied at the Paris Conservatory and won the much-sought "Prix de Rome." With the possible exception of **Richard Strauss** (strouss), he is the most talked-about composer living. His fame has come largely through his success in leaving beaten paths and making melodies and harmonies that have a very new flavor. Some of his effects are very beautiful, but the newness of the harmonies makes it difficult for us to accustom our ears to them. His opera *Pelleas and Melisande* is his best-known work, although he has written much for orchestra and for the piano.

Gustave Charpentier (shar-pahn'-tiay), born at Dieuze, France, 1860 (still living), is a striking composer of dramatic music, whose opera *Louise* has been a sensation both in Europe and in America. His other works are not so well known. He is a graduate of the Paris Conservatory and a pupil of Massenet. He also won the "Prix de Rome."

Paul-Marie-Theodore-Vincent d'Indy (dan'-dy), born in Paris, 1851 (still living), is one of the most distinguished of the French composers of to-day. He was a pupil of Franck and his works are well known in all musical countries. His best works are for orchestra, and the most famous is probably a *Symphonie upon the Air of a French Mountaineer.*

Theodore Clement-François Dubois (doo-bwah'), born in Rosnay, France, 1837 (still living). Pupil of Ambroise Thomas at the Paris Conservatory and winner of the "Prix de Rome." In 1896 he became director of the Conservatory, succeeding Thomas. His works for the opera, the church and the concert-room show able musicianship and deep musical feeling.

Alexandre Felix Guilmant (geel-mong), born at Boulogne, France, 1837 (still living), is the greatest of French organ performers and the composer of much remarkably fine music for this instrument.   Guilmant has toured America twice, as well as England, Italy and Russia.   He held the position of organ professor at the Paris Conservatory for a number of years.

Charles M. Widor (vee'-dor), eminent organist and composer, born at Lyons in 1844.   Pupil of Lemmens and Fétis.   He was appointed professor of organ at the conservatory in 1890, and of counterpoint and fugue in 1896.   His ten symphonies for organ are very famous.

Paul Dukas (du'-kah), born at Paris in 1865.   Famous composer and critic.   Pupil of the Paris Conservatory.   Best known by his very successful opera *Ariane et Barbe-bleue* (Bluebeard).

TEN TEST QUESTIONS.

1. Why was Paris important as a musical city?
2. When and where was Berlioz born?
3. How did Berlioz support himself while studying at the conservatory?
4. What is the famous prize known as the "Prix de Rome"?
5. In which way did Berlioz extend the use of the orchestral instruments?
6. Give a short description of the life and work of Charles Gounod.
7. Give a short description of the life and work of Ambroise Thomas.
8. Give a short description of the life and work of Camille Saint-Saëns.
9. Tell something of the work of Debussy, Massenet and Charpentier.
10. Tell something of the work of Cesar Franck, Theodore Dubois, Vincent d'Indy, Alexandre Guilmant, Charles Widor and Paul Dukas.

JOHANNES BRAHMS.   EDVARD GRIEG.
JOSEPH JOACHIM RAFF. CARL H. REINECKE.   ANTONIN DVŎRÁK.
PETER ILJITCH TCHAIKOVSKY.   MORITZ MOSZKOWSKI.

LESSON XXXI.

MASTERS AT THE CLOSE OF THE NINE-TEENTH CENTURY.

WE HAVE already studied about the great French composers who are either living now or whose greatest work was done during the last one hundred years. Let us now learn something of the great masters who occupied similar positions in other nations. An entire lesson might readily be devoted to the masters of Russia, another to the masters of Germany, Austria and Bohemia, and yet another to the Scandinavian musicians (Norway, Denmark and Sweden). However, since our object is now to get a knowledge of the *main* factors in the advance of music, only confusion could result from an attempt to describe the many worthy but lesser-known composers. These may be studied to far better advantage when you have become familiar with the main outlines of musical history, and you should not neglect to continue your studies with a more advanced work.

As you come to study the music of the composers of different nations, you will see how the characteristics of the people of the nation enter into the work of the composers. The German people, for instance, are noted for their substantial, thorough methods and for their simple, homely rules of life, while the Russians have tendencies toward the deep and sombre in life. The French are vivacious and brilliant. The Scandinavian nations regard life in a much bolder and more rugged manner.   Thus, although one might think that the great composers who preceded those we are to study now could have left but little work for these masters to do, it is marvelous how these national tendencies have brought out much that is new and beautiful.   The works of **Tchaikovsky** (chy-koff'-skee), for instance, are filled with magnificent combinations of tones, and the works of Brahms were so masterly that when his first symphony was produced it was called *The Tenth Symphony,* meaning that it was worthy of being classed with Beethoven's immortal nine.

Johannes Brahms (bramz), born in Hamburg, Germany, 1833; died in 1897.   His father was a player in a theatre orchestra, and Brahms received his first instruction from Eduard Marxsen in the neighboring city of Altona.   From him Brahms received such a thorough training in pianoforte playing and composition that when he was twenty years old he made tours with the violinist **Remenyi** (reh'-men-yee) and aroused the interest of Liszt and Schumann.   Schumann heralded Brahm's talent from the same generous motives that led him to spread wide the fame of Chopin.   In 1862 he settled in Vienna and remained there practically all the remainder of his life, working in peace and quiet, and occasionally conducting important concerts of orchestras and singing societies.   Although some musicians regard Brahms' works as dull and "leaden," he could compose music that was very sprightly and invigorating.   Some of his Hungarian dances were examples of this.   His tendency was toward the classical, and the critics of the day fought a merry war of words over the attempt to determine whether Brahms or Wagner was the greater composer.   The fact of the matter was that these two great men had very different purposes and there was no basis upon which to decide such a question. Brahms' principal works include two fine pianoforte concertos, four remarkable symphonies, many fine smaller works for piano, and a choral work entitled *The German Requiem.* Brahms gave great attention to detail and his works show this finish to an unusual degree.

Peter Iljitch Tchaikovsky (chy-koff'-skee), born at Wotkinsk, Russia, 1840, died in 1893, was unquestionably the greatest of Russian composers, although his style is blended with that of the composers of other European nations and is said to be less dependent upon the folk-songs of the Russian people than the music of some other Russian composers. Tchaikovsky was originally intended for the law, but when he was twenty-two he entered the St. Petersburg Conservatory, which had been founded by Anton Rubinstein. In 1866 he became instructor of harmony at the Conservatory and held this position for eleven years. After this time he gave his attention almost entirely to musical composition and produced works of richness and beauty which have made his name immortal. He is particularly great in his works for orchestra and his symphonies, particularly the fifth and sixth, are in great demand at concerts. His twelve operas are little known outside of Russia, but his other orchestral works, his piano concertos and his songs are widely known and much admired.

Edvard Hagerup Grieg (greeg), born in Bergen, Norway, 1843, died in 1907, stands foremost among the composers of Scandinavia. His first lessons were from his mother. In 1858 he entered the Conservatory at Leipzig and studied there for four years. A few years later he studied under Gade, in Copenhagen. Grieg became an able pianist and made several tours, but in 1880 he settled in Bergen and his tours became less frequent, owing to ill health. Many people regard Grieg as one of the lesser composers because he wrote so many short pieces for the piano, but musicians consider him in an entirely different light and look upon him as one of the very greatest modern masters. His knowledge of the technic of composition and his employment of harmony were masterly in the extreme. Aside from his exquisite pieces for pianoforte and his beautiful songs, he is best known for his suite for orchestra, called *Peer Gynt* (pare gint), three fine violin sonatas, and a pianoforte concerto of great melodic and harmonic charm.

Antonin Dvorak (tfor'-shak), born in Mühlhausen, Bohemia, 1841, died in 1904, is looked upon as the greatest of Bohemian composers. His father was an innkeeper, who wanted his son to be a butcher. He learned how to play the violin from the schoolmaster in his town, and when he was sixteen he left home and went to study the organ in the Bohemian capital, Prague. He supported himself by playing in a small orchestra. After leaving the school he became a viola player in the orchestra of the National Theatre. His works did not attract any general attention until he was thirty-two years of age, when one of his compositions was produced which aroused such wide interest that the Government provided him with an annual sum of money to assist him in continuing his work as a composer. Grieg's works are strongly marked with the characteristics of the folk-songs of Sweden and Norway, and Dvôrák's works are accordingly marked with the characteristics of Bohemian national melodies. He has written nine Bohemian operas, but is best known in other countries by his symphonies, his *Stabat Mater,* his oratorio *St. Ludmilla* and his very fascinating songs.

Moritz Moszkowski (mosh-koff'-skee), born at Breslau, 1854 (still living), is of Polish origin. He studied at home and at the Dresden Conservatory and at the conservatories of Stern and Kullak (kool-lakh) in Berlin. He made several successful tours as a pianist. His very attractive pieces for piano, especially his concert valses, his *Serenata* and his *Spanish Dances* have made his work very popular among pianists.

Joseph G. Rheinberger (Ryne'-bayr-ger), born Vaduz, Austria, 1839, died 1901. He was an eminent organist and composer, but was even more famous as a teacher of composition.

Max Bruch (brooch), born at Cologne, 1838 (still living), a very able composer, now teacher of composition in the Royal High School of Music at Berlin. His first symphony was produced when he was only fourteen. His most famous works are his violin concertos and his choral compositions. Bruch's compositions are scholarly and yet are filled with novel, sound combinations and melodic interest.

Karl Goldmark, born at Keszthely, Hungary, in 1830 (still living). Eminent violinist, pianist and opera composer. Studied in Vienna as a young man, but is chiefly self-taught. His most celebrated compositions are orchestral and dramatic. His opera, The Queen of Sheba, was produced in 1875.

TEN TEST QUESTIONS.

1. Tell how the racial tendencies of different peoples affect the music of a nation.
2. Who wrote what was called the *Tenth Symphony?*
3. Tell something of the work of Brahms.
4. Tell something of the works of the man who is looked upon as the greatest of Russian composers.
5. Give a short description of the life of Grieg.
6. Give a description of the life of Dvôrák.
7. For what is Moszkowski particularly famed?
8. Tell something of the work of Goldmark.
9. In what capacity was Rheinberger most famed?
10. In which great institution is Bruch now engaged as a teacher?

Mrs. H. H. A. Beach.   Liza Lehmann.

Carl Löwe.

Hugo Wolf.   Robert Franz.

LESSON XXXII.

THE MODERN ART-SONG AND ITS COMPOSERS.

WE LEARNED in our lesson upon the Troubadours and the Minnesingers that many of the tunes which they composed became familiar to the people and were sung so frequently that they were called people's songs or folk-songs. Other songs written by hundreds of unknown composers, some of whom possessed no more musical ability than the natural talent for making a simple melody set to some words written by a local poet, also became popular. These folk-songs represented the traits and the feelings of the people from whom they sprang. Great composers have used them as parts of their own compositions; that is, they would use a folk-song as a theme for one of the movements of a sonata or a set of variations. Beethoven, Brahms, Tschaikowsky, and, in fact, nearly all our great composers, were not above using these melodies freely. These folk-songs were often works of great melodic beauty.

The folk-song, however, does not represent the highest in the art of song. Other composers found that the plan of repeating the same melody for every stanza, as is done, for instance, in the case of the hymn, was not suitable to some forms of poetry. The song in which the music was repeated for each stanza was called a *Strophic,* and the new plan of changing the music to suit the poetry was called by the Germans "durch componiert" (through-composed), and is known in other countries as the *Art-song.*

Although composers named **Miller, Reichardt** (ry-kart), **Schulz, Zumstieg** (tsoom-steeg), and others had written many beautiful songs, as indeed had the great masters Haydn, Mozart and Beethoven, the art-song came into prominence with the works of Franz Schubert, who showed a most wonderful genius in this style. Others of the great composers whom we have already studied have written beautiful songs of the art-song type. The most noted in this list are Schumann, Liszt, Brahms, Grieg, MacDowell, Rubinstein, Tschaikowsky, Debussey and Strauss. Many other composers, however, have shown a special fondness for songs and are more famed for works of this kind than for their other compositions. The following are the best-known composers of this class:

Karl Löwe (leh'-veh), born in 1796 at Löbejün (leh'-beh-yeen), died in 1869, is best known as the perfecter of the ballade. The ballade in the sense of an art-song is a musical setting of some stirring legend of considerable length. Löwe's best-known ballades are *Edvard, Goldschmiedstochterlein* (The Goldsmith's Little Daughter), *The Erl-king* and *Archibald Douglass*. Löwe wrote many lengthy works, including seventeen oratorios and one opera. He was a fine singer and did much to introduce his own works. He was also a man of wide culture and received the degree of doctor of philosophy from Griefswald University.

Robert Franz (frahnts), born in 1815 at Halle, Germany, died 1892, was a wonderfully gifted composer of songs. His real name was Knauth, but he had this changed in 1847 to Franz. In his youth he made exhaustive studies of Bach, Handel, Beethoven and Schubert, but at first met with little success with his own compositions. However, a set of songs written in 1843 attracted the attention of Schumann, Mendels-

ENRICO CARUSO.
    LILIAN NORDICA.   ADELINA PATTI.
        ERNESTINE SCHUMANN-HEINK.

MADAME MELBA.
    MARCELLA SEMBRICH.
        LUISA TETRAZZINI.

sohn and Liszt, and he met with the good fortune of becoming an organist of one of the leading churches of Halle, director of the Academy of Singing and musical director of the University of Halle. He wrote, in all, three hundred and fifty songs, and these were so remarkable that it is said they were among the few works which won the enthusiastic admiration of Richard Wagner. Franz, unfortunately, was seized with sickness and deafness in 1868, and had it not been for his friends in Germany and in America, who collected twenty-five thousand dollars for his benefit, he and his gifted wife, who also wrote excellent songs, would have suffered greatly.

Hugo Wolf (vohlf), born in 1860 at Windischgratz (vindish-grats), Styria, died in 1903, was a composer of some of the most artistic settings of the poems of Goethe (gehteh) and others. His works created a great sensation in Germany, and Hugo Wolf Societies were formed to give them recognition. He also wrote a symphonic poem, a light opera and some fine chamber music. He was unable to save his earnings and was given to worrying about his inability to make a living. This resulted in insanity. He was regarded as one of the most talented song writers since Schubert and Schumann.

Adolf Jensen (yen'-sen), born in 1837 at Königsberg, died in 1879, was largely self-taught. He hoped to study with Schumann, and went to Russia to earn money to enable him to do this, but Schumann's death prevented their meeting for this purpose. For a time he directed a theatre in Posen, and later taught in Tausig's school in Berlin. He published about one hundred and sixty songs of high artistic value. He also wrote many charming works for orchestra, and many excellent piano pieces.

Eduard Lassen (lahs'-sn), born in 1830 at Copenhagen, died in 1904, was a pupil of the Brussels Conservatory and must have been a very brilliant student, since he carried off several prizes. He was appointed music director at Weimar in 1858, and became Liszt's successor in 1861. Here he produced Wagner's *Tristan and Isolde* in 1874. This was considered a remarkable achievement, since the opera had been given but once before (in Munich), and had been abandoned as "too difficult" at Vienna. Lassen wrote four operas and much successful music for the orchestra. His songs, although not so deep in character as those of some of the great song writers, have been extremely popular, and he is best known to-day through them.

Other song writers who have attained eminence through frequent representation upon concert programs are the Germans Alexander von Fielitz and Eugen Hildach, the Frenchmen Paul Vidal, Emile Paladilhe, and Reynaldo Hahn (born in Venezuela), the English composers Amy Woodforde Finden, Liza Lehmann, Maud Valérie White, and Landon Ronald.

TEN TEST QUESTIONS.

1. What is said to have been the source of many of the folk-songs of France and Germany?

2. How have the great masters employed folk-songs?

3. What is a strophic song?

4. How does the strophic song differ from the modern *Art-song?*

5. Name some very great masters who have written songs.

6. Describe a ballade, and give the name of the composer who was famed for writing them.

7. Tell something of the work of Robert Franz.

8. Tell something of the life of Hugo Wolf.

9. Which great song writer desired to study with Schumann?

10. Which famous Wagnerian opera did Lassen produce at Weimar?

WILLIAM MASON. ISIDOR PHILIPP.

THEODOR KULLAK. THEODOR LESCHETIZKY. SIGISMUND THALBERG.

HANS VON BÜLOW. L. M. GOTTSCHALK.

LESSON XXXIII.

SOME FAMOUS PIANISTS AND PIANO TEACHERS OF THE NINETEENTH CENTURY.

WE HAVE now learned of most of the great masters whose works brought them wide fame prior to the beginning of the present century, with the exception of a very modern group of composers, as well as our American composers and some who are perhaps better known as pianists. Music depends upon interpretation, "the art of bringing the meaning of the composer into existence in tones," and the composer must always be subject to the whims of the interpreter or performer. Several of these interpreters or virtuosos, however, were so important as composers that it is hard to decide in which class to place them.

Sigismund Thalberg (tahl'-bairg), born in 1812 at Geneva died in 1871, was considered one of the greatest rivals of Franz Liszt. He studied in Vienna with Hummel and **Sechter** and **Mittag.** His tours in Europe and in North and South America were enormously successful. He was a very brilliant performer and was the originator of the style of composition in which the theme was ornamented by variations consisting of arpeggios continually running from one end of the pianoforte to the other. He wrote over sixty-six works, but few of them are heard to-day.

Louis Moreau Gottschalk, born in 1829 at New Orleans, La., died 1869, was a pupil of **Halle, Stamaty** and **Madalen** in Paris. At the age of sixteen he made highly successful tours in European countries. In 1853 he came back to America and played in all parts of the United States with great success. His style was greatly appreciated by American audiences of the day, with the result that while some of his pieces are very well known, many of Gottschalk's best works are insufficiently appreciated. As a performer, Gottschalk had a peculiar style all his own, and those who were familiar with his playing contend that few artists since his time have approached him in charm of rhythm or "velvety" tone. Gottschalk was also very popular in South America.

Henri Herz (hairts), born in 1806 at Vienna, died in 1888, was a pianist of ability and was for many years professor of pianoforte at the Paris Conservatory, of which he had previously been a pupil. He was one of the most successful composers and performers of his day, but, because he bent too much to popular taste and wrote in the empty, frivolous, fashionable style, his compositions are now almost unknown, although he received for them sums far above the amounts paid to the best composers of his time. He toured in America (1845-1851), and later settled in Paris as a manufacturer of pianos.

Theodor Kullak (kool'-lak), born in 1818 at Krotoschin, Posen, died in 1882, was one of the foremost musical educators of the past century. His father desired him to be a physician, and Kullak studied medicine in Berlin, but finally gave it up to be a musician. His teachers were Czerny, Sechter, **Nicolai,** Dehn and **Agthe.** His first piano tour in Austria made him famous as a thoroughly trained and gifted artist. He later settled in Berlin, becoming court pianist and teacher to the royal family. Here he was one of the founders of the Stern Conservatory, and later established a very famous school of his own, called "The New Academy for Tonal Art."

Among Kullak's pupils are **William Sherwood,** Moritz Moszkowski, and the famous Viennese pianist, **A.** **Grünfeld**
(green-felt).   Although he wrote many pianoforte pieces, he
is best known by his famous and widely used *School of
Octave Playing.*

   Karl Klindworth (klint-vort), born in 1830 at Hanover,
is better known as a teacher and an editor than as a virtuoso.
He was a pupil of Franz Liszt, and he taught with great success in London, Moscow and Berlin.   In the latter city he
founded a conservatory with the co-operation of Von Bülow.
This conservatory has since united with the famous Scharwenka (shar-ven'-ka) Conservatory.   Although he wrote very
few original compositions, his piano arrangements of the
Richard Wagner music dramas and his careful editing of the
works of Chopin and Beethoven give him high rank in the
musical world.

   Theodor Leschetizky (leh-shay-tit'-skee), born in 1830 at
Lancut, Austrian Poland, is one of the greatest of all piano
teachers.   He was a pupil of his father and of Czerny and
Sechter.   After many successful tours as a virtuoso, he
settled in St. Petersburg as a teacher at the Conservatory.
In 1880 he went to live in Vienna and met with tremendous
success as a teacher.   Among his pupils are Paderewski,
Essipoff, Bloomfield-Zeisler, Gabrilowitsch (ga-bree-lo'-
vitsch), **Hambourg, Katherine Goodson** and many other
virtuosos.

   Adolph Bernhard Marx (marks), born in 1795 at Halle,
died in 1866, was very celebrated as a musical educator.   His
compositions were uninspired, but his great activity as a writer
upon educational subjects and musical theory made him a very
important figure in the musical history of the past century.

William Mason, born in 1829 at Boston, died in 1908, was a pianist, composer and musical educator whose splendid work entitles him to rank with the greatest European teachers and artists in his line. He was a son of **Dr. Lowell Mason,** one of the foremost of early American musicians. His pianoforte and theoretical studies were pursued under Moscheles, Hauptmann, **Richter, Dreyschock** (dry'-shok), Liszt and others. His playing abroad and in America pronounced him a virtuoso of the highest class. He wrote many charming compositions, but his best-known work is *Touch and Technic,* a system of pianoforte study which has been highly praised by **Joseffy** (yo-séf-fee), Paderewski, Liszt and others. Associated with Dr. Mason in his educational work in America have been **W. S. B. Mathews** and **E. M. Bowman,** whose ability as educators has brought them national fame.

Isidor Philipp (fil-leep'), born in 1863 at Budapest, is a pupil of **Mathias,** Chopin's famous disciple; Saint-Saëns, Heller and **Ritter.** He is an able pianist and one of the leading teachers of the Paris Conservatoire. His charming piano pieces and his technical works are well known.

TEN TEST QUESTIONS.

1. What famous pianist was born in New Orleans?
2. What style of composition did Thalberg originate?
3. Why did the works of Herz gradually fall into disuse?
4. Who was the famous German pianist who later became celebrated as a teacher in Berlin and founded "The New Academy for Tonal Art"?
5. For what is Klindworth particularly celebrated?
6. Name a celebrated theorist whose writings had wide influence?
7. Which American pianist became very famous through his educational work?
8. With whom did William Mason study?
9. Which famous pianist has reached great fame as a teacher of virtuosos?
10. For what is Isidor Philipp particularly celebrated?

LESSON XXXIV.

GREAT VIRTUOSOS OF THE PRESENT DAY.

WE HAVE now learned of the pianists and piano teachers who have had a wide influence as teachers and composers; let us now consider some famous performers upon the piano, many of whom also have reputations as composers and as educators, but who are best known as virtuosos. In order that you may fix these great players more clearly in your mind, we will study them in groups, as taught by their famous masters.

LISZT'S PUPILS.

We have already learned of Liszt's famous pupils, Von Bülow, Raff, Klindworth, Mason and others. The ones we are to consider now are hardly less famous.

Eugen d'Albert (dal'-bair), born in 1864 at Glasgow, Scotland, although famous for years as a virtuoso, has recently won new fame as a composer of the successful opera *Tiefland*. He is a pupil of **Pauer, Stainer, Prout** and **Sullivan** in London, Richter in Vienna, and Liszt in Weimar. His playing is strong, brilliant, and his technic remarkable.

Emil Sauer (sour), born in 1862 at Hamburg, was a pupil of his mother, then of Nicholas Rubinstein and finally of Franz Liszt. Sauer has not achieved great fame as a composer, but his playing is so remarkable that many consider him the greatest living virtuoso. His playing is poetical, yet vigorous, and shows a finely balanced artistic feeling.

Moritz Rosenthal (ro'-sen-tahl), born in 1862 at Lemburg, a pupil of **Mikuli** (mee-koo'-lee), a pupil of Chopin, Joseffy and Franz Liszt. His technic is phenomenal and he is a virtuoso of the very highest rank.

William H. Sherwood, born in 1854 at Lyons, New York, is a pupil of Dr. Mason, Theodor Kullak, Deppé, Liszt and many others; highly successful as a virtuoso both in Europe and in America. He is a finished, scholarly player and an able teacher. He died January 1, 1911.

Other very famous pupils of Franz Liszt include: B. J. Lang, Reisenauer (ry'-sen-au-er), Bendel (bend'-dl), R. Burmeister, A. Friedheim, Adele Aus der Ohe (oh-eh), Sophie Menter, D. Pruckner, Meyer-Olbersleben, Sgambati (sgam-bah'-tee), Siloti, Stavenhagen, Karl Tausig (tow-sig), Emil Liebling, Edward Baxter Perry, Richard Hoffman.

LESCHETIZKY'S PUPILS.

Ignace Jan Paderewski (pah-der-ef'-skee), born in 1859 in Podolia, Poland, is the most famous living pianist; pupil of **Raguski** (rah-goos-kee) in Warsaw, of **Wuerst** (veerst) and **Urban** in Berlin, and of Leschetizky in Vienna. He is enormously successful in the United States and in England. His playing is reposeful, yet strong and vigorous; artistic, yet full of deep feeling and character. No virtuoso has ever had a greater power over audiences. His compositions include one opera, a symphony, and many fine pianoforte compositions.

Fannie Bloomfield-Zeisler (tseys'-ler), born in 1866 at Bielitz, Austria, was brought to America at the age of two, and was educated in this country. She ranks with Paderewski

Eugen d'Albert.

Teresa Carreño.

Xaver Scharwenka.

Vladimir de Pachmann.

Josef Hofmann.

Moritz Rosenthal.

as one of Leschetizky's greatest pupils.   She is received with
the highest enthusiasm by audiences in all parts of Europe
and America, and is comparable with the greatest performers
of all time.   She has made two highly successful European
tours.

Ossip Gabrilowitsch (ga-bree-lo-vitsch), born in 1878 at
St. Petersburg, was a pupil of both Rubinstein and Leschetizky.   He is a very finished and poetical player, who has
met with wide popular favor in America and in Europe.

Other famous Leschetizky pupils who are known in the
United States are Katherine Goodson, Mark Hambourg, An-
nette Essipoff (ess'-i-poff), whom Leschetizky married, and
Slivinski (slee-vin'-skee).

PUPILS OF OTHER NOTED TEACHERS.

Josef Hofmann (hoff'-man), born in 1877 at Cracow,
Russia, was a pupil of his father, who was the teacher of
harmony at the Warsaw Conservatory.   Later he studied
with Rubinstein.   At the age of nine he astonished the musical world with a phenomenal tour of the great cities, after
which he went into retirement, and again made his appearance
at the age of seventeen, and has since won wide recognition
by his masterly playing.

Teresa Carreño (car-rehn'-yo), born in 1853 at Caracas,
Venezuela, a pupil of Rubinstein, Gottschalk and Mathias, and
a performer of wonderful skill, insight and force.   She has
been received in all the great cities of the musical world on
equal terms with the foremost virtuosos of our time.

Xaver Scharwenka (shar-ven'-ka), born in 1850 at Sam-
ter, Poland, is a pupil of Kullak, and has made highly successful tours in Europe and America.   He is now one of the

IGNACE PADEREWSKI. WILLIAM SHERWOOD.
FANNIE BLOOMFIELD-ZEISLER.
HAROLD BAUER. EMIL SAUER.
OSSIP GABRILOWITSCH.

heads of the Scharwenka-Klindworth Conservatory in Berlin. His compositions are many and include a fine pianoforte concerto, a symphony and an opera. His *Polish Dance* is one of the most widely known pianoforte pieces.

Vladimir de Pachmann (pahk'-mahn), born in 1848 at Odessa, has made a specialty of Chopin's works and is unexcelled in the performance of them. He was a pupil of his father, and of **Dachs** at the Vienna Conservatory. Notwithstanding many eccentricities, he is a very great artist.

Raoul Pugno (poon'-yo), born in 1852 at Montrouge, France, is a brilliant pianist and a broad musician. He studied at the Paris Conservatory and took in succession the first prizes in piano, organ and harmony. In 1896 he became a professor of piano at the Conservatory. His compositions are quite numerous and show decided originality.

Leopold Godowsky (god-off'-skee), born in 1870 at Wilna, Russian Poland, is a pupil of the Royal High School of Music in Berlin. Later he studied with Saint-Saëns in Paris. He made two tours of America and taught in this country for several years. Returning to Europe, he met with still greater success as a teacher in Berlin and Vienna. His technic is so great that many feel he has reached the limit of human ability in this direction.

Harold Bauer (bower), born in 1873, at London, England, studied violin with his father and with A. Pollitzer, and made tours of England as a violinist for nine years. He determined to become a concert pianist and went to Paris to study with Paderewski. After only one year of study he toured Russia as a concert pianist and has since toured most of the countries of Europe and America with huge success. Bauer has a fine intellect and a very poetical nature, and his recitals have an appeal to the music-lover as well as the student.

Ferrucio Busoni (fare-rutch-chio boo-so'-nee), born in 1866 at Empoli, Italy, was first taught by his parents, who were both musicians, and later under W. A. Remy in Graz. His playing shows great breadth and a finely trained mind. His compositions and his arrangements of the works of Bach are excellent. Busoni taught for a time at the New England Conservatory, and has made many tours in Europe and in America. He ranks as one of the foremost masters.

Rafael Joseffy (yo-séf-fee), born in 1853 at Hunfalu, Hungary, was a pupil of Moscheles and Reinecke at the Leipsic conservatory, and of Tausig in Berlin. His delicacy of touch, combined with a very remarkable technic and musicianly understanding, made him one of the foremost virtuosos of our time. For over twenty years Joseffy has resided in America as a teacher.

Sergei V. Rachmaninoff (rach-mahn'-een-off), born in 1873 at Nijni-Novgorod, Russia, graduated from the conservatories of St. Petersburg and Moscow; pupil of **Siloti** (see-loh'-tee), **Arenski** and **Taneieff**. Although he has made successful tours as a pianist and as a conductor, he will be best known as a composer. Many look upon him as the greatest Russian since Tschaikowsky. His *Prelude in C Sharp Minor* is enormously popular. In 1910 he became the supervisor of all the leading conservatories of Russia.

Thirty-five of the great virtuoso pianists mentioned previously in this book have toured America. A great number of them have spent some years in this country as teachers. The result is that the standard of pianoforte playing in America is now as high as in any country in the world. This also

applies to pianoforte teaching, since during the past fifty years
we have not only had the advantage of instruction from great
European virtuosos who have been resident in America, but
also from remarkably capable American teachers who have not
been content to investigate the systems of one country alone,
but who have received instruction in many leading European
music centres.   The American musician has distinguished himself in educational work, and in several European cities American teachers may be found among the most successful
musicians.

TEN TEST QUESTIONS.

1. Name at least ten famous pupils of Franz Liszt.
2. Which famous German pianist is considered by many as the greatest
virtuoso of our time? *Emil Sauer .*
3. Give the name of an American pupil of Liszt who has achieved fame
both in America and in Europe. *Sherewood*
4. For what is Rosenthal particularly famed? *His technic is phenomenal*
5. Who is the most successful of all living virtuosos? *Paderewski*
6. Which woman pupil of Leschetizky is regarded as one of the foremost living pianists? *Fannie Zeisler .*
7. Tell something of Leschetizky's other famous pupils. *Gabrilowitsch*
8. Name the countries in which the following famous pianists were
born: Hofmann, Carreño, Scharwenka, De Pachmann, Pugno, Godowski,
Bauer, Busoni, Joseffy. *Hungary*
9. Give the name of the best-known teacher of each of the foregoing.
10. Which famous pianist was a successful violinist before studying
piano?

LESSON XXXV.

GREAT VIOLINISTS OF THE PAST AND PRESENT.

In Lesson XII we learned of the great makers of the violin who lived in the seventeenth and eighteenth centuries. While there has been an immense improvement in the manufacture of the piano and the organ, the violin remains practically the same. In fact, the violins of **Stradivarius** (strah-dee-vah-ree-us) and other makers bring higher prices to-day than ever. Consequently, violinists have had a perfect instrument to work with, and the art of playing the violin has not been influenced by the improvement of the instrument, as is the case with the piano.

Among violin virtuosos one great figure stands out above all others, and there seems to be no disputing the fact that the greatest violinist of all was **Niccolo Paganini** (pah-gah-nee'-nee), born in 1782, at Genoa, Italy; died in 1840. His father, a poor shopkeeper, taught him to play the mandolin and provided him with the best teachers his limited means would permit. When he was eight he composed a sonata for the violin and when he was eleven he played in public with great success. His youth was marred by his drunken habits and his fondness for gambling. Nevertheless, his genius was so great that even these terrible enemies of success did not defeat him. When he was twenty-two he started upon a tour of the countries of northern Europe,

which was practically a triumphal procession. Everywhere
he outdid his rivals with ease, and his technic was so mar-

PAGANINI PLAYING THE VIOLIN.

Paganini led a wild and intemperate life, and at one time was confined in
prison, where he whiled away his time playing his favorite violin for the benefit
of the other convicts.

velous that he was thought by the peasants in some districts
to be in league with the evil one. No difficulty seemed too
great for him, and he allowed his playing to be carried away

JOSEPH JOACHIM.

FRITZ KREISLER.

HENRI WIENIAWSKI.

EUGENE YSAYE.

JOHANN KUBELIK.

MISCHA ELMAN.

by his emotional feeling until audiences were dazzled and bewildered by the effects he produced.   His compositions, although useful for the violinist, do not compare in importance with his playing.

Other violinists who did not arouse such sensational interest as Paganini have, nevertheless, been great virtuosos and many of them have produced works for the violin far greater than those of Paganini.   Among them are:

Charles de Beriot (beh-ree-o), born in 1802 at Louvain, France, died in 1870, was a pupil of **Viotti** (vee-ot′-tee) and **Baillot** (bai-yo).   His tours of Europe were unusually successful.   He married Mme. **Malibran** (mah′-lee-bran), who was one of the most famous singers of the time, and he was deeply devoted to her.   For nine years he was professor of violin playing at the Brussels Conservatory, and besides writing valuable educational works he composed seven violin concertos and many other pieces which are widely used by violinists.

Ole Bull (o-leh bool), born in 1810 at Bergen, Norway; died in 1880.   Although he was said to be lacking in the qualities of finished musicianship, his technic and method of playing his own compositions were so unusual that he was received with great favor by popular audiences.

Ferdinand David (dah′-veed), born in 1810 at Hamburg, Germany, died in 1873, was a pupil of Spohr and Hauptmann. He was a virtuoso of high order, and as director of the Gewandhaus Orchestra and teacher in the famous Leipzig Conservatory he stood in the very first rank.   He wrote numerous compositions of educational value for violinists.   He was the teacher of **Wilhelmj** (vil-hel′-mee) and **Joachim** (yo-a′-kim).

Joseph Joachim (yo-a'-kim), born in 1831 at Kittsee, Austria, died in 1908, commenced his lessons at five and played in public at seven. He studied with **Boehm** (behm) in Vienna and with David in Leipzig. For a time he held posts as concertmeister, first at Weimar (vi'-mar) and then at Hanover. In 1868 he was appointed head of the "Royal High School of Music" in Berlin, and the present status of the school as one of the leading musical institutions of Germany is due in a large measure to Joachim's hard work and untiring enthusiasm. So finished and forceful was his playing that he earned the popular title of "The King of Violinists." The string quartet of which he was the leading spirit, and which was known as the "Joachim Quartet," was the standard quartet of the world for many years. Joachim was an admirable composer for the violin and devoted his life solely to what he believed to be the best and noblest in music.

Henri Vieuxtemps (vee-oo-tom'), born in 1820 at Verviers, Belgium, died in 1881, was a virtuoso and teacher whose works have made him doubly famous. He toured at the age of eight, and when visiting different cities endeavored to continue his musical education. Everywhere his playing was greatly admired. He visited America three times. In 1846 he was appointed court violinist to the Czar of Russia and became professor of violin playing in the St. Petersburg Conservatory. Later he taught in the Brussels Conservatory. His compositions, which include six concertos, are highly valued by violinists.

Henri Wieniawski (vee-nee-av-skee), born in 1835 at Lobin, Poland, died in 1880, was a pupil of the famous violin teacher **Massart** at the Paris Conservatory. His tours took him to all parts of Europe and America. For a time he

HENRI MARTEAU.

MAUD POWELL.

PABLO DE SARASATE.

HENRI VIEUXTEMPS.

NICOLO PAGANINI.

taught at the St. Petersburg Conservatory, and in 1874 he succeeded Vieuxtemps as professor of violin playing at the Brussels Conservatory. His tone was rich and broad and his technic striking. His tour of America with Rubinstein was of great artistic benefit to the country.

August Wilhelmj (vil-hel'-mee), born in 1845 at Usingen, Nassau, died in 1908, was described by Liszt as "a second Paganini." He studied with David, Hauptmann, Richter, and later with Raff. He made many extremely successful tours, including a four-year tour of the world in 1878. In 1894 he became professor of violin playing in the Guildhall school of music in London and remained in the English capital until his death.

Pablo de Sarasate (sah-rah-sah'-teh), born in 1844 at Pamplona, Spain, died in 1908, played so remarkably at the age of ten that Queen Isabella presented him with a fine Stradivarius violin. From his twelfth to his fifteenth year he studied at the Paris Conservatory, taking the first prize. He combined great natural talent for the violin with a thorough training and a high order of musicianship, so that several musicians wrote famous pieces for him, such as the *Second Concerto* of Bruch. Although he wrote comparatively little, his pieces are frequently played by violinists.

So many are the violinists of the present day that we can only mention a few and tell of their teachers.

Eugene Ysaye (e-sah'-ee), born in 1858 at Liege, Belgium; pupil of Liege Conservatory and of Wieniawski and Vieuxtemps; now among the very greatest living violinists.

Maud Powell, born in 1868 at Peru, Ill.; a pupil of Joachim and others. Her immense success abroad, as well as in this country, entitles her to recognition among the foremost of the world's violinists.

Fritz Kreisler (kreys'-ler), born February 2, 1875, at Vienna; pupil of Delibes and Massart at Paris; immensely successful in both Europe and America.

Henri Marteau (mahr'-toh), born in 1874 at Rheims, France. Studied at the Paris Conservatoire and won first prize in 1892. Has toured Europe and America. Succeeded Joachim at Berlin Royal High School.

Johann Kubelik (koo'-be-lick), born in 1880 at Michle, Hungary; pupil of Sevcik (save-chick) at the Prague Conservatory; has since toured the great cities of Europe and America, creating astonishment everywhere by his marvelously perfect technic.

Mischa Elman (el'-man), born in 1891 at Talnaje, Russia; pupil of Auer. In a comparatively few years this son of a poor Jewish schoolmaster has become one of the foremost violinists of the age.

Limitations of space enable us to give only the birth dates of the following eminent violinists: E. Remenyi, 1830; Mme. Normann-Neruda (Lady Hallé), 1839; E. Sauret, 1852; O. Musin, 1854; Marie Hall, 1884; and Francis Macmillan, 1885.

TEN TEST QUESTIONS.

1. Who is looked upon as the greatest of violin virtuosos?
2. Tell something of the bad habits which led to Paganini's misfortunes.
3. Why was Paganini thought to be in league with the devil?
4. In what great school did Ferdinand David teach?
5. Tell something of the career of Vieuxtemps.
6. With which great pianist did Wieniawski tour America?
7. Give some facts about Joachim's career.
8. What did Liszt call Wilhelmj?
9. Give some facts about Sarasate's career.
10. Name the country in which the following were born: Ysaye, Kubelik, Maud Powell, Ole Bull.

LESSON XXXVI.

COMPOSERS OF VALUABLE PIANOFORTE PIECES IN SMALLER FORMS.

WE HAVE learned of the very great masters of the past, and now we shall turn our attention to composers who are best known for their efforts as makers of smaller musical art works. We cannot measure an art work by its size. A painting covering a whole wall, by Michael Angelo (mee'-kale an-jeh-lo), is not necessarily greater because of its size than a picture by the artist Velasquez (veh-las-kase), which might only be a foot square. Thus, the *Songs Without Words* of Mendelssohn and the shorter pieces of Chopin and Brahms are in many cases greater artistically than some symphonies by less able composers. The following composers have in some cases written with marked ability in the larger forms, but their smaller compositions have brought them their widest reputation:

One of the best-known writers of shorter compositions for the piano is **Cécile Chaminade** (shah-mee-nád), born in 1861 at Paris. She is the first musician of her sex to attain wide renown as a composer. Clara Schumann, Robert Schumann's wife, was well known as a virtuoso and wrote several excellent works, but they never met with anything like the general popular appreciation that has greeted the charming piano pieces of Chaminade. She was a pupil of Lecouppey (le-coop-pay), Savard, Marsick and Benjamin

Godard. Her best-known work is the ballet-symphonie *Callirhoe* (cal-lìr-o'-eh), which was filled with such original and fascinating musical ideas that it won her wide fame. As a composer of songs, Chaminade stands with the best composers of her native country. She has toured abroad and in America with great success.

Benjamin Godard (go-dahr), born in 1849 at Paris; died in 1895, was a most talented and successful composer of pieces in the smaller forms. Almost everything Godard had to say in his music was interesting, and his compositions are filled with lovely melodies and attractive rhythmic forms. At first he was a violinist and played in public at nine. Later he studied with the great violinist Vieuxtemps. His first published work was a violin sonata, and he followed this with much attractive chamber music. Godard wrote eight operas, of which the best known is *Jocelyn* (jos-lin). He also wrote many pieces for the orchestra and some very fascinating pieces for piano, including the immensely popular *Second Mazurka*.

Franz Bendel (ben'-del), born in 1833 at Schoenlinde, Bohemia, died in 1874, was a pupil of Franz Liszt. He was highly regarded as a pianist. In 1862 he became one of the leading teachers in Kullak's academy in Berlin, and wrote many pieces which are valuable to some students, since they are melodious, yet not difficult.

Christian Sinding (sind'-ing), born in 1856 at Königsberg, Norway; pupil of Reinecke at Leipzig Conservatory; studied later in Berlin, Munich and Dresden. Although Sinding is best known by his poetical and artistic piano pieces, such as the famous *Frühlingsrauschen* (Rustle of Spring), he is a composer of great ability in the larger forms, and has written

CHRISTIAN SINDING.   BENJAMIN GODARD.

CECILE CHAMINADE.

EDUARD SCHÜTT.   LUDWIG SCHYTTE.

THEODORE LACK.

a symphony, a pianoforte concerto and many works for orchestra that rank with the best of their kind.

Eduard Schütt (sheet), born in 1856 at St. Petersburg. Like Sinding, he is known by his lighter works, but has written masterly works in larger forms, his pianoforte *Concerto in G Minor* being among his best compositions. Schütt was a pupil of the St. Petersburg Conservatory and the Leipzig Conservatory, and in later years became a deep personal friend of Leschetizky in Vienna, where he resides. Schütt's *Carnival Mignon* is an extremely attractive concert number, and his valse *À la bien Aimée* is one of the most popular piano compositions ever written.

Ludwig Schytte (skit-tay), born in 1850 at Aarhus, Denmark, was at first a druggist, but at twenty decided upon a musical career. His teachers included Neupert (noy-pehrt), Gade and Liszt. In 1887 he went to Vienna as a concert pianist, composer and teacher, and has written a great number of original and charming pieces for the piano, of which the most popular is his *Berceuse* (Lullaby). He died in 1909.

Theodore Lack (lähk), born in 1846 at Quimper, France, studied at the Paris Conservatory with **Marmontel** and **Bazin,** and now resides in Paris as a teacher and a composer. His known works are limited to very attractive salon (parlor) pieces, of which the most successful is, perhaps, the *Idylle* (e-dill) in A flat.

Paul Wachs (vachs), born in 1851 at Paris, was also a pupil of the Paris Conservatory, where he studied with Masse (mass-ay), Marmontel, Cesar Franck and Duprato. In 1872 he won the first prize for organ playing. His brilliant pianoforte pieces, including the widely played *Shower of Stars* have won him wide popularity.

Leo Delibes (deh-leeb'), born in 1836 at St. Germain-du-Val, France, died in 1891, has written some of the most melodious and brilliant ballet music we possess. The ballet is a form of stage dance usually employed in connection with an opera. Sometimes ballets are given separately, and they often include pantomimes or plays accompanied by music and dancing, but without singing or speaking. Delibes was a graduate of the Paris Conservatory and later in life became professor of composition in that institution. Pieces from his captivating ballets *Naila, Coppelia* and *Sylvia* are well known, through much-played pianoforte arrangements. Of his six operas, the best known is the beautiful *Lakme*.

Johan Severin Svendsen (svent'-sen), born at Christiania, Norway, in 1840, died June 14, 1911. Able violinist, composer and conductor, studied at Leipsic Conservatory. Made extensive tours as a virtuoso. Wrote much remarkably individual music including symphonies and concertos. His best known piano piece is *Winter*, and his *Romance* for violin is played by all violinists.

TEN TEST QUESTIONS.

1. Who was the first woman to attain international renown as a composer? *Chaminade - Born in Paris.*
2. What instrument did Godard play? *Violine Born in Paris.*
3. Which pupil of Liszt became famous for his short pieces, and later taught in the Kullak Music School? *Franz Bendel - Born in Bohemia*
4. Give the name of an eminent Norwegian composer who has become famous for his shorter piano pieces. *Christian Sinding*
5. What is Schütt's most famous composition? *Concerto in g minor*
6. Give the name of an eminent Danish composer who has written in smaller forms. *Schytté*
7. Where was Theodore Lack educated? *Paris (on) Born in Quimper*
8. With which great organist did Paul Wachs study? *Massot. Born in Paris*
9. For what style of music is Delibes famous? *Ballet*
10. In which famous conservatory did Delibes become the teacher of composition? *Paris Conservatory.*

when S Svendsen, Born at norway -

HANS ENGELMANN.

CORNELIUS GURLITT.

CARL BOHM.

PAUL WACHS.

FRANZ BENDEL.

CARL HEINS.

LESSON XXXVII.

COMPOSERS OF INSTRUCTIVE PIANOFORTE PIECES IN SMALLER FORMS.

Too great stress cannot be laid upon the importance of the composers of instructive pianoforte pieces in smaller forms. Without pieces of this class, we can easily see how difficult and unpleasant the way of the beginner in music would be made. It is, of course, possible to undertake the early study of music by using technical exercises and studies such as those of Cramer, Clementi and Czerny and others, but teachers to-day realize that the taste of the pupil must be developed, and in many cases this is best accomplished by the use of the little pieces of such composers as the following. These compositions are often bridges from the dryness of pure technical work or from music commonly called "trash" to music of a more difficult and complicated nature. Many of the following composers have written little gems for the beginner:

Cornelius Gurlitt (goor'-litt), born in 1820 at Altona, Prussia, died in 1901, was a pupil of the father of Carl Reinecke for six years. Gurlitt was an intimate friend of Niels W. Gade. For a time he resided in Copenhagen, then in Leipzig, and later in Rome. In the latter city he studied painting. Finally he located in Altona as a teacher and was very successful. Later he became famous as the conductor of a military band. He wrote a vast number of compositions, including operas, cantatas and symphonies. He is best known, however, for his very excellent teaching pieces, in which he combines pretty melodies with sound musical knowledge.

Louis Köhler (kay'-ler), born in 1820 at Brunswick, Germany, died in 1886, was educated in Brunswick and Vienna, and after holding two positions as a theatrical conductor he finally settled in Königsberg, where he met with great success as a teacher and as an author of enormously successful educational works for the piano. He wrote three operas and was the first teacher of the famous pianist **Reisenauer** (ry'-senour).

Carl Bohm (bome), born in 1844 at Berlin, has written many very interesting songs and pianoforte pieces. He is a pupil of **Loeschhorn** (lesh'-horn), Reissman and Geyer, and his compositions, particularly his song *Calm as the Night,* have met with wide popularity. His most successful pianoforte pieces are *The Silver Stars, La Vivandiere* and *La Zingara.*

F. Behr (bare), born in 1837 at Mecklenburg, died in 1898, wrote particularly tuneful pieces for children in the early grades of music. Although many of these were published under his own name, he also wrote much under the assumed names of "Wm. Cooper," "Charles Morley" and "Francesco d'Orso." His most popular piece is *The Camp of the Gypsies.*

Gustav Lange (lang'-eh), born in 1830 at Erfurt, Germany; died in 1889. He wrote over four hundred pieces. He was an exceedingly modest man and his tastes were for music of the highest and best, although his own works rarely rose above the drawing-room grade. His *Flower Song* is one of the most popular of all the lighter pianoforte pieces.

Georges Bachmann (bahk'-mahn), born in 1848 at Paris, France, died in 1894, wrote inspiriting pianoforte pieces which, although simple technically, sound somewhat difficult and very brilliant. His most popular piece is *Les Sylphes*.

Hans Engelmann (en'-gel-mahn), born in 1872 at Berlin, Germany, is the son of an officer in the German Army, who later became private secretary to the German emperor William I. He had the best instruction obtainable in his youth, studying in both Leipzig and Berlin. Engelmann came to America in 1891 and went directly to Philadelphia, establishing himself as a teacher. He is one of the most prolific of all composers of salon or drawing-room music. His published compositions alone number over twelve hundred. A wonderful sense of melody combined with the art of making his compositions at all times thoroughly playable for the student has made his pieces, such as *Melody of Love* and *When the Lights Are Low,* extremely popular.

Carl Heins (hines), born in 1859 at Tangermünde, like Engelmann, seems to have an inexhaustible spring of pretty melodies. He studied the violin and the cornet when a boy, but later devoted his attention to composition, studying at the Leipzig Conservatory under **Radecke, Taubert,** Dorn and others. Later he studied voice with **Stockhausen.** He now resides in Berlin as a teacher of vocal and instrumental music. His teaching compositions are valuable because they combine exercises in technic with the sugar-coated form of pieces.

Ignace X. J. Leybach (li'-bach), born, 1817, in Alsace, then France, now a part of Germany; died in 1891; was a pupil of Kalkbrenner and Chopin. Aside from being a successful pianist in his day, he was also an excellent organist and held the post of organist at the Toulouse Cathedral. He wrote an organ method, some songs, and brilliant, showy pianoforte pieces, including the famous *Fifth Nocturne*.

Heinrich Lichner (lickh'-ner), born in 1829 at Harpersdorf, Silesia, died in 1898, studied in Berlin and Breslau with excellent teachers.   In Breslau he became an organist of local renown, but he is best known by his lighter pianoforte pieces, which, although lacking the character and finish of the works of some other composers of such pieces, nevertheless became very widely used.

TEN TEST QUESTIONS.

1. Which famous composer of shorter pieces was also a painter?
2. Who was the teacher of Reisenauer?
3. Name some of Carl Bohm's most popular compositions.
4. Which composer employed many assumed names?
5. What kind of man was the composer of "The Flower Song"?
6. Name the brilliant Parisian composer who wrote "Les Sylphes."
7. Who is one of the most prolific composers of drawing-room music?
8. Tell something of Carl Heins.
9. With whom did Leybach study?
10. For what is Heinrich Lichner famed?

LESSON XXXVIII.

MUSIC IN AMERICA.

WHEN the Puritans came to America in 1620, music in Europe was really quite advanced, although Bach and Handel were not born until sixty-five years later. At first the strict religious beliefs of the Puritans limited the music of the Colonies to psalm tunes, but about one hundred years later (1717) we find singing schools and choirs springing into existence. About the middle of the eighteenth century the interest in music greatly increased, and **William Billings** (born in 1746 at Boston) has the reputation of being the first American composer of renown. His compositions were very crude, however, and woefully behind those of the leading musicians in Europe, since they were of necessity limited to hymn tunes and bungling musical settings of religious texts.

In the first part of the eighteenth century musical societies were formed, the most noted being the "Stoughton (Mass.) Musical Society," which had grown from a singing class formed by Billings in 1774, and the "Handel and Haydn Society," formed in Boston in 1815. Soon thereafter, musical and orchestral societies sprang into existence in New York, Philadelphia and other cities, and it is somewhat surprising to learn that Beethoven's *First Symphony* was performed by the Musical Fund Society in Philadelphia as early as 1821. Opera had been given in New Orleans, New York and Philadelphia still earlier. In 1825 **Manuel Garcia** (gar-chee-ah) brought an excellent opera company to New York, which included his daughter, Mme. Malibran, and his son, Manuel Garcia, Jr., who became one of the world's most famous singing teachers and lived to the age of one hundred and two.

One of the greatest forces in early American musical history was **Lowell Mason** (born in 1792 at Medfield, Mass.; died in 1872), who, although almost entirely self-taught, did more for the advancement of music in America than any other musician of his time. As a young man he conducted choirs in Medfield and at Savannah. In 1827 he became president of the Handel and Haydn Society of Boston, and ten years later he went abroad to study musical teaching methods. He published many popular collections of music for the home and choir, which brought him a very large income. In Lesson XXXII we have already learned of the excellent work of his son, William Mason.

Theodore Thomas (born in 1835 at Essen, Germany; died in 1905), following Dr. Lowell Mason, was a very powerful factor in the development of music in America. He studied the violin with his father and played in public at six. At the age of ten he came to America and made important tours of the country as a violin virtuoso. Thomas conducted different orchestras at different times in New York, Brooklyn and Cincinnati, and later became conductor of the famous Chicago Orchestra, which after his death was named the "Thomas Orchestra." Thomas was very advanced in his views, and the excellence of his programs won him fame in Europe.

Dr. Leopold Damrosch (born in Posen, 1832; died in 1885), at first a physician and later an able violinist and conductor, came to America in 1871. He had been an intimate

DUDLEY BUCK.   HORATIO PARKER.
ETHELBERT NEVIN.   EDWARD A. MacDOWELL.   ARTHUR W. FOOTE.
       G. W. CHADWICK.   J. K. PAINE.

friend of Liszt and Wagner, and his services in introducing the works of modern masters in America cannot be over-estimated. This work has been ably continued by his sons, **Frank Damrosch** and **Walter Damrosch.**

John Knowles Paine (born, 1839, at Portland, Maine; died in 1908) was one of the first American musicians to show the results of thorough European schooling. He studied with Kotschmar at Portland, and with Haupt (howpt), Fischer and Wieprecht at Berlin. He was an exceptionally fine organist and played with success in Europe and in America. In 1876 he became professor of music at Harvard, and held this position until his death. His works, which include two symphonies, two symphonic poems, an oratorio, a mass, and other notable works, are scholarly and dignified, yet show deep musical feeling. **Dudley Buck** (born in 1839 at Hartford, Conn.), pupil of Plaidy, Moscheles, Hauptmann, J. Rietz in Liepzig, and later of Schneider in Dresden, stands with J. K. Paine and William Mason as one of the pioneers of advanced musical work in America. He was a very excellent organist, and after his return to America he continually held fine organ positions in many of the representative churches of the country. For a time he was assistant conductor to Theodore Thomas. His compositions have been exceptionally popular and, possibly, have sold better than those of any other American composer with serious intentions. They include much excellent organ music, many fine cantatas and numerous exceedingly popular works for the church choir. All of his music shows his sensitive, intensely musical nature. He died October 6, 1909. **Benjamin J. Lang** (born in 1837 at Salem, Mass., died in 1909), also had the advantage of European study in the day when European study was a neces-

sity.   He was a pupil of his father, of Alfred Jaell (yale) and
of Franz Liszt.   In addition to being an able organist, he was
also a very fine pianist and a most excellent teacher. He settled
in Boston and was the conductor of many important societies,
including the "Handel and Haydn" Society.   His compositions include symphonies, overtures, an oratorio and much
church music.

The more modern composers in America have not attempted
to found an American school differing widely from the music
of the European masters, but have tried to create works which
shall rank with the best of European composers.   There
seems to be little difference of opinion among critics in placing Edward MacDowell at the very head of American composers of recent years.   **Edward MacDowell** (born in 1861
at New York, died in 1908) was a pupil of Teresa Carreño,
J. Buitrago and P. Desvernine in New York, Marmontel and
Savard at the Paris Conservatory, and Heymann and Raff
at Frankfurt.   In 1881-1882 he was the head teacher of
pianoforte in the Darmstadt (Germany) Conservatory.   For
some time he lived in Wiesbaden, Germany, and in Boston,
but in 1896 he was appointed professor of music at Columbia
University, New York.   He made several concert tours and
revealed himself as a virtuoso of the highest type.   His compositions are strikingly original, full of deep musical feeling
and character, and show a very comprehensive knowledge of
the technic of musical composition.   They include almost all
forms, and have met with wide appreciation notwithstanding
their lofty musical style.   Owing to worry and overwork,
MacDowell suffered from a mental trouble in later years which
made death a blessing.   **George Whitfield Chadwick** (born
in 1854 at Lowell, Mass.) was an organ pupil of Eugene

Thayer in Boston, Reinecke and Jadassohn (yah'-das-sone) in Leipzig, and Rheinberger in Munich.   For many years he has been a successful organist in Boston and has been director of the New England Conservatory of Music since 1897.   His compositions for orchestra, church and the voice all show strength and musical skill combined with decided talent.

Horatio W. Parker (born in 1863 at Auburndale, Mass.) was a pupil of Stephen Emery, J. Orth and G. Chadwick at Boston, and of Rheinberger and Abel in Munich.   Parker is an able organist, a choirmaster, and has held some of the most desirable positions in America, but he is best known as professor of music at Yale University, a position which he has held since 1894, and as a composer.   His works, which embrace oratorios, cantatas, a symphony, worthy organ compositions and excellent songs, show breadth and finished musicianship.   His oratorio *Hora Novissima* (ho-ra no-vis'-si-ma), which was given at an important festival at Worcester, England, was one of the first large compositions of an American to attract attention in Europe.   **Arthur W. Foote** (born in 1853 at Salem, Mass.) has received his musical education entirely in America.   He is a pupil of Lang, Emery and Paine in Boston.   His works show a natural ability to create beautiful melodies and indicate that in finish and thoroughness he has lost nothing by failing to go abroad.   His orchestral pieces, cantatas, songs and piano compositions are fascinating and often powerful.   **Ethelbert W. Nevin** (born in 1862 at Edgeworth, Penna., died in 1901), one of the most melodious and artistic of all American composers, confined himself almost entirely to the shorter forms and rarely attempted to produce scholarly or deep musical works; nevertheless, his very great talent and originality, as well as his fine taste, place him among the leading American song writers. His piano pieces, such as the famous *Narcissus* and the *Barchetta* (bar-ket'-ta) from *May in Tuscany,* have sold enormously. He was a pupil of Heide and Gunther in Pittsburg, Pearce, Lang and Emery in Boston, Boehme in Dresden, and Bülow, Klind-worth and Bial in Berlin.

Mrs. H. H. A. Beach (born in 1867 at Henniker, N. H.), although a piano pupil of Perabo and Baermann, and a har-mony pupil of J. W. Hill, is almost entirely self-taught in counterpoint, composition and orchestration. Her numerous compositions include symphonies, concertos and cantatas, as well as many exceedingly beautiful pieces in smaller forms. Mrs. Beach's works all show lofty ambition and musical talent of masterly character. Her symphonies have been performed by the Boston Symphonic Orchestra with great success.

William W. Gilchrist (born in 1846 at Jersey City, N. J.) is a pupil of Dr. Hugh A. Clarke, of the University of Penn-sylvania. He has held important posts as organist and has written choral and church music, as well as songs of a very high order.

No account of American music would be complete without some mention of **Stephen C. Foster** (born in 1826 at Law-renceville, Penna.; died in 1864), who, although self-taught, had the wonderful power of writing truly beautiful melodies which have been so much sung by the American people that they have reached the rank of folk-songs. They include *The Old Folks at Home, My Old Kentucky Home* and *Old Black Joe.*

There are other composers who have lived in America whose compositions have been immensely popular with the people. Among them we may mention **John Philip Sousa** (born in

15

1856 at Washington, D. C.), famous as a bandmaster and the author of marches that have been played more than the works of any other American composer; **Reginald de Koven** (born in 1859 at Middletown, Conn.), composer of many successful light operas. **Victor Herbert** (born at Dublin, February 1, 1859). Although born in Ireland, Herbert has resided in America nearly a quarter of a century and has done the better part of his work here. He commenced his musical education in Germany at the age of seven, and became a violoncellist of marked ability. His first engagement in America was as solo cellist at the Metropolitan Opera House in New York. Since then he has been engaged as a band conductor and as an orchestra conductor. His greatest success, however, has been in writing the music for comic operas, which have brought him enormous popularity and a large fortune. The limitations of space prevent our giving detailed biographies of such worthy American composers as James H. Rogers, Harry Rowe Shelley, E. R. Kroeger, Emil Liebling, H. W. Loomis, H. H. Huss, Margaret R. Lang, Ruben Goldmark, R. H. Woodman, Whitney Coombs, Wilson G. Smith, Arthur Farwell and many others.

TEN TEST QUESTIONS.

1. Who was the first American composer of national fame?
2. Describe the development of the singing societies from the early singing schools.
3. Tell something of the excellent work done by Lowell Mason.
4. Was Theodore Thomas born in America?
5. Why is Theodore Thomas so famous?
6. In which great university did J. K. Paine teach?
7. For what was Dudley Buck famed?
8. Give an account of the education and works of Edward MacDowell.
9. Tell something of the work of the most famous woman composer of America.
10. Give some fact connected with the life and work of G. W. Chadwick, H. W. Parker, Arthur W. Foote, E. W. Nevin, W. W. Gilchrist, Stephen C. Foster and other composers mentioned in this lesson.

LESSON XXXIX.

SOME MASTERS OF TO-DAY.

AFTER Wagner, Liszt and Brahms had passed away, many felt that the limits of music had been reached and that no new composer would arise with the bravery to attempt new effects that would differ from those of Wagner and his rivals, but Debussy (deh-bus'-see), about whom we have already studied, and Richard Strauss are now exciting as much interest as did Wagner, Liszt and Brahms in their day.

Richard Strauss (strouss), born in 1864 at Munich, who is in no way connected with the famous Viennese family of waltz composers, has astonished the whole musical world by his wonderful ability in counterpoint and orchestration. His works are often so intricately written that many people are unable to understand and appreciate them. They contain evidences of the master of the highest description. His father was a performer upon the French horn, and his first and only lessons were received from **W. Meyer.** He commenced composing at a very early age and attracted the attention of Von Bülow and Lassen. Strauss has held many very important posts as music director (kapellmeister) in Munich, Weimar and Berlin and has shown high ability as a conductor. His first works to attract wide attention were his symphonic poems, such as *Don Juan* (don hoo-an'), *Death and Transfiguration, Till Eulenspiegel's* (oy-len-spee-gel) *Merry Pranks, Thus Spake Zarathrustra, A Hero's Life* and *The Domestic Symphony.*

These works were in a sense a triumph for the ideas of Wagner and Liszt, since they were written in the free style of the symphonic poem which Liszt employed and were in the class of "program music" which Wagner advocated. Each poem is supposed to represent in tone the musical ideas that passed through the composer's mind as he thought of the poem or legend which inspired him to write the symphonic poem. It is impossible to tell a story or a legend in music, but if the story is already known it is interesting to know of the musical ideas that passed through the composer's mind when he had the same story in view. Music that follows a set story, legend or idea of this kind is called "program music." Program music is not new, as some of the very ancient writers employed the idea, but it has been used more in the last century than ever before. Strauss' songs have attracted wide attention, but his greatest fame has come through the operas *Feuersnot, Salome* (salo-meh' or sa-lo'-meh) and *Elektra,* which have been discussed by the newspapers of the entire world.

Max Reger (ray'-gher), born in 1873 at Brand, Germany, has received almost as much attention in his native land as Strauss. He is a pupil of **Lindner** and **Hugo Riemann,** and was for a time professor of music at the Leipzig University. His works are very numerous and in almost all styles, and show wonderful contrapuntal skill.

Edward Elgar (born in 1857 at Broadheath, England), is, without doubt, the greatest English composer since Purcell and one of the foremost masters of the day. He is almost entirely self-taught, and he held many small musical posts before he gained recognition. His works include a symphony, many choral and orchestral works and oratorios, two of which, *The*

S. Coleridge-Taylor.　　　　　　　　　Max Reger.

Richard Strauss.

Edward Elgar.　　　　　　　　　　　Jean Sibelius.

Dream of Gerontius and *The Apostles,* have won him world-wide fame. He was knighted in 1904.

Other English musicians whose works entitle them to be classed as masters are: **Sir Arthur Sullivan** (born in 1842 at London, died in 1900), composer of wonderfully successful and artistic comic operas (*The Mikado, Pinafore,* etc.), as well as a grand opera and some fine church music. **Sir Alexander Mackenzie** (born in 1847 at Edinburgh) is the principal of the Royal Academy of Music and a composer of great talent.

Sir Hubert Parry (born in 1848 at Bournemouth), director of the Royal College of Music, is a scholarly writer and the author of many excellent musical books. **Sir Charles Villiers Stanford** (born in 1852 at Dublin) is a fine teacher and conductor, as well as a gifted composer. **Frederic H. Cowen** (born in 1852 at Kingston, Jamaica, West Indies) was educated in England and Germany and his works have met with great popular success. **Samuel Coleridge-Taylor** (born in 1875 at London) is considered the greatest of negro composers. His works are very modern in their style, and his *Scenes from Hiawatha* is one of the best cantatas known for small choral societies. **Sir John Stainer** (born in 1840 at London, died in 1901), was one of the most successful writers of English church music. **Sir Joseph Barnby** (born in 1838 at York, died in 1896, was an able conductor, organist and composer of church music. **Michael William Balfe** (born in 1808 at Dublin, died in 1870), considered by many the greatest of Irish composers, was at first an operatic baritone and later a composer. While his works lack great skill and depth, he had a marvelous talent for making lovely melodies. Balfe's best known work is *The Bohemian Girl.* **William Vincent Wallace** (born in 1814 at Waterford, Ireland; died in 1865) was a very gifted Irish composer, whose opera *Maritana* was extremely successful.   **Jean Sibelius** (see-bay'-lee-oos), born in 1865 at Tavastehus, Finland, is considered the foremost composer of Finland, which is now a part of Rsssia.   He is a pupil of **Goldmark.**   He wrote one of the first Finnish operas, *The Maid of the Tower.*   His later orchestral works met with wide favor.

In the study of advanced musical history you will learn of many other noted men and women who are now producing fine musical works.   It is better not to try to carry too many names in the mind at one time, and there are many composers about whom you can find out in musical dictionaries and encyclopedias.   You will also find that, in order to gain a really good idea of musical history, you will have to review what you have studied many times.   Before you study an advanced work you will find it far better to master this book thoroughly. If you once have the main facts so thoroughly fixed in your mind that you can answer any important question intelligently, you will find that your interest in all the music that you play or which you may hear will be very greatly increased.

TEN TEST QUESTIONS.

1. Do the works of Richard Strauss rank with those of the greatest masters?

2. State the three classes of music in which Strauss has won wide fame.

3. Give a simple description of program music.

4. Tell something of Max Reger.

5. Who is the greatest English composer since Purcell?

6. Name six famous English composers.

7. Who is considered the greatest composer of the negro race?

8. Name two Irish composers of operas.

9. Who is considered the foremost composer of Finland?

10. Should this book be mastered thoroughly before an attempt is made to study some advanced work?

LESSON XL.

A SUMMARY OF MUSICAL HISTORY.

THE object of this lesson is to give a summary, or condensed account, of musical history, so that you can get the outlines clearly fixed in your mind. In so very short a lesson it is evident that only the most important facts can be presented.

Before the birth of Christ we have observed that the ancient peoples of Asia and southeastern Europe and Egypt practised musical art, and that the highest development of this art took place in Greece, where scales similar to our minor scales came into use.

The next step in the advancement of music was made by the early Catholic Church, in the service of which music became a very important part. Singing schools were founded and scales were devised similar to those of the Greeks. The church fathers also devised a system of musical notation which was of immense importance to all future musical effort.

About the twelfth century the knights of northern and southern France devoted themselves to the art of music and became wandering minstrels. They wrote and composed songs which in many cases became part of the folk-song or people's song of the country. These noble singers were called "troubadours" or "trouvères." In Germany a similar movement started a little later, differing somewhat from that in France, but much the same in purpose. The German singers were called "minnesingers." Later, in Germany, clubs of workingmen formed themselves into singing societies and became known as "mastersingers." The last guild of master-singers went out of existence in 1836.

The greatly increased interest in music led to the art of combining two or more melodies to be sung at the same time, called counterpoint or polyphonic writing. The first master of this art was said to have been John Dunstable, who died in 1453. Many famous writers of polyphonic music followed Dunstable, among whom Orlando Lasso and Palestrina deserve particular attention. The latter did much to reform the music of the mass of the Roman Catholic Church and became very famous.

In 1595 an Italian priest named Filippo Neri formed a society known as the "Congregation of the Oratorio," which was devoted to the presentation of Biblical plays accompanied by music. These came to be known as "oratorios." About the same time a society of gentlemen in Florence devoted themselves to the presentation of plays upon non-Biblical subjects, and these came to be known as "operas." Many famous musicians developed these forms, among whom were Monteverde, Alessandro Scarlatti, Jean Baptiste Lully and Jean Philippe Rameau.

Late in the seventeenth century we note a vast improvement in the organ and the violin, as well as the invention of the pianoforte. This made a great impression upon the music of future composers.

With the advent of the great composer Johann Sebastian Bach, in 1685, we mark the highest step in the art of polyphony, while with his famous contemporary, George Frederic Handel, born in the same year, we find an important advance in the art of opera writing, as well as the development of the oratorio. With Haydn, Mozart and Beethoven, the classical forms known as the sonata and the symphony reached their highest mark. Mozart's operas in the meantime had met with huge success, and the works of Gluck had revolutionized ideas of opera construction by making the music more dependent upon the meaning of the verbal text.

After the classical composers we reach Weber, Mendelssohn, Schubert, Berlioz and Schumann, all of whom showed tendencies to break away from strict set laws and follow their own musical bent by creating new laws to govern new musical conditions. Chopin and Liszt, both of whom gave most of their attention to the piano, were still more liberal in their musical views and paved the way for the wonderful work of Richard Wagner, whose ideas upon music were so very different from those of all his predecessors that he practically created a new school, a school which has influenced all the greater composers who have followed him.

After Wagner, such composers as Grieg, Verdi, Tschaikowsky, Brahms, Dvorak, Elgar, Strauss, MacDowell, Debussy and others, have brought musical art to its present highly advanced stage.

APPENDIX—I.

HOW TO ORGANIZE A YOUNG FOLKS' MUSICAL CLUB.

TEACHERS and those interested in musical education are of one mind regarding the effectiveness of the "Young Folks' Music Club" movement which has become so popular throughout our country during the last twenty-five years. The idea of associating entertainment with study, which is the foundation of so many educational systems, needs no endorsement in these days. Practical experience has shown that music study and musical pleasure cannot be combined in any more profitable manner than through the medium of the "Young Folks' Music Club." Musical incentive, competition, sociability, united effort and, in fact, all advantages of the class system combined with private instruction are open to the teacher who employs the musical club idea in her regular work. The testimony of thousands of teachers who have conducted clubs for years is that they would feel greatly handicapped if they did not have some such means of developing the auxiliary musical work of their pupils.

The organization of a musical club is a comparatively simple matter, but so many are the mistakes which, if made at the beginning, may ruin a club, that it is well for the teacher to consider the details of organization very carefully. If it is desired to have the membership composed solely of the pupils of the teacher, the one consideration is age and musical ad-

vancement.   Most teachers find it desirable to have either
two musical clubs or one club with a junior division and a
senior division.   Still others who conduct kindergarten classes
conduct kindergarten clubs.

The writer's personal experience leads him to believe that a
safe age for division is about thirteen or fourteen.   Children
of thirteen or fourteen are not sufficiently matured in their
ideals to look down upon children of eight or ten.   However,
the child of fifteen is inclined to regard those under thirteen as little children and resents being associated with them.
Young people from fourteen to eighteen usually come together
on the same social basis in a musical club.   This represents
the "high school" age, when the individual desires personal
recognition and is above the discipline of the child.   Of course,
no set age limit can be made, as much depends upon the men-
tality and intellectual maturity of the member.

SOCIAL CONDITIONS.

The teacher may also be obliged to consider social conditions.   In some localities the conditions are so heterogeneous
that a club is almost impossible.   People of a priggish or snob-
bish nature resent having their children associate with anyone but those whom they personally select.   Here the teacher's
tact must come to the front and the desirability of the musical
club must be forcefully presented and the thought that the
child of the snob can be injured by association with the more
plebeian pupil, soundly ridiculed.   When the music club has a
definite purpose and the leader keeps the workers intelligently
and actively engaged, the idea of class distinction disappears.

At the first meeting it is usually wise to determine upon a

meeting-place. The idea of meeting at the homes of the different members is not usually a good one. The fact that one member has a more bountifully furnished home than another is liable to cause jealousy and dissatisfaction upon the part of the less fortunate members of the club. Moreover, the members will do better work if they are not obliged to work in new and different surroundings at each meeting. If the teacher or club leader has a bright, cheery, sunshiny room with a piano and the requisite musical books, no better meeting-place could be desired.

SELECTING THE OFFICERS.

At the first meeting the officers of the club should be selected. The inclination will be to make the teacher president. This, of course, should be avoided and the teacher should be classed as a leader rather than as a president. This important office should be reserved for one of the members. A knowledge of parliamentary law is not required, and the teacher can instruct the "president" elected in the simple duties of his office, such as "calling the meeting to order," "ordering the minutes read," "taking a vote," "adjourning the meeting," etc. The treasurer should also be selected from the club members and taught the necessity of keeping strict account of all fees and dues received from club members. The secretary of the club should be one of the older members who can write intelligently and who has the time to send out club notices. These officers should be elected at the first meeting, but the politic teacher should have no difficulty in having her own candidates elected without the pupils becoming conscious of her electioneering efforts.

The teacher who assigns but three offices is running the danger of engendering jealousy upon the part of the other members. The member who has an office always takes a more active part. The only solution is to create offices, as was done in the old Polish nobility, when it was said that every man in seven had been created a nobleman. This can be done in the music club by forming committees. There may be a "Reception Committee," to receive the guests at the "open meetings" of the club; an "Entertainment Committee," to look after the games at the club meetings; a "Membership Committee," to go through the formality of determining upon new members; a "Refreshment Committee," to take charge of any refreshments served at the meetings, and a "Program Committee," to discuss the matter of the club programs with the teacher. The teacher or club leader will find that many young folks have a great fondness for "red tape" of this kind. Nothing delights them more than to go through the same proceedings that they have been led to believe their elders employ at their club meetings.

Naming the Club.

This is a much more important matter than many might imagine. To secure a name that is both attractive and simple is not easy, because so many names have been used that it is hard to find a new one. The names of localities make desirable names for musical clubs; for instance, "The Stuyvesant Heights Musical Club," "The Rittenhouse Musical Club," "The Beacon Musical Club," "The Woodside Avenue Musical Club." Other club leaders lean toward names of the great composers, such as "The Beethoven Club," "The Mozart

Club," "The Chaminade Club," "The MacDowell Club," etc. Musical terms have also been widely employed, such as "The B Sharp Club," "The Allegro Club," "The Andante Club," "The Presto Club" and "The Etude Club." (Owing to the great popularity of *The Etude,* hundreds of highly successful "Etude Clubs" have been formed all over the country.) The main idea in securing a name is to avoid taking a name with a high-sounding and lofty significance, quite beyond the understanding of the people of the district in which the club is located. Such names as "The Fortissimo Musical Club," "The Rimsky-Korsakoff Musical Club" or "The Polyphonic Musical Club" are obviously bad for a young folks' musical organization, because they are too hard to pronounce, too little understood and too high-sounding.

The First Meeting.

The meetings of a young folks' musical club should never be lengthy. The writer has found that one hour and a half is adequate. If the pupils show an inclination to stay longer they should be discouraged, since it is far better to have them end the session with a desire for more than to have them leave "bored" or tired out.

After the meeting has been called to order, the leader should explain the advantages of a musical club, and make it very clear that the main purpose of the club is to study, although a great many good times will be sandwiched in. Following the custom of clubs in general, it is the practice to attend to the business of the club at the beginning of the meeting. This should be followed by the study division or the principal part of the meeting.

The Study Section.

It should be the club leader's main aim to make the study section of the meeting the most interesting part of the work of the club. Otherwise, the very purpose of the club will be defeated. Various branches of musical education may be taken for study, but "musical history" is by far the most popular. Every child who studies music should have a knowledge of the history of the art. This knowledge will add fifty per cent. to the interest and enjoyment the child will derive from music in after-life. It spares the child the humiliation which historical ignorance often brings when the topic of music is brought up in society. The foregoing history lessons are simply intended to give young people the most vital facts in as interesting and clear a manner as the limitations of the work will permit. The teacher should, however, be awake to every idea to make the meetings more interesting. It will pay the club leader to search libraries for good anecdotes of the composers discussed, to get all kinds of little bits of musical information to tell the young folks at the club meetings. This work is planned to provide the backbone, without which the study cannot be continued. It remains for the teacher to add the necessary zest and individual character to the meeting.

One excellent plan is by means of contests. The children, for instance, may be requested to write compositions upon some special branch of musical history. The teacher should offer a prize or a series of prizes for the winners of the contest. An excellent prize is a plaster cast of the bust of some favorite composer. Any really good musical book may be used as a prize, and it is by no means absolutely necessary to have the prizes of an exclusively musical nature. Here are some topics for compositions:

"How the troubadours and minnesingers differed from the meistersingers."

"Bach and Handel."

"How the opera came to be."

"The story of the pianoforte and some of its masters."

After the study section, which may last from half an hour to forty-five minutes, the entertainment part of the club meeting should come. This may be treated in many different ways. Games may be provided, or a good musical program may be arranged in which the members may take part. If the teacher has some musical friend who will attend the meeting and play or sing, as an added feature, the members will appreciate this. In the warm days of the spring it is wise to plan some excursions to neighboring woods or places of interest.

Every effort should be made to promote sociability. The members should be encouraged to assist other members in their work, and the friendly spirit should be cultivated. One of the most successful musical clubs in the world is the club known as the "St. Cecilia," in Grand Rapids, Mich. This is a club of ladies, and it is cited here because the work of the club is noteworthy for its many excellent charitable undertakings.

CLUB EXPENSES.

The fees of the club should be made as low as possible. The best way to decide upon a fee is to estimate the regular running expenses of the club, add a margin for safety, and then apportion the amount according to the membership of the club. For instance, the expenses might be:

For prizes, etc. $0.50	per	meeting
For refreshments .... .50	"	"
For decorations, etc. .... .25	"	"
For stationery, postage, etc. .... .25	"	"
For extras .... .25	"	"

$1.75

In a club of twenty members the fee would, therefore, be about ten cents per meeting. The only initiation fee should be that for the purchase of the requisite study material. Each individual member of the club should have a book. It is a bad plan to try to do with too few books, as the pupils lose interest because the difficulty in securing information becomes too great. This is especially necessary in the study of history, harmony, biography, etc. Some teachers add to the gross expenses a small fee of ten or twenty cents per lesson for each pupil for services in conducting the history or harmony class or club. Since these are studies which cannot be pursued without the assistance of the teacher, and since the teacher has in almost every case been obliged to pay for her own instruction in these subjects at a very much higher rate, this course seems justifiable.

It frequently happens that at the end of the season sufficient funds are left over to enable the members to procure tickets for some local concert or operatic performance, when the club may go as a body.

APPENDIX—II.

HINTS ON CONDUCTING A YOUNG FOLKS' MUSICAL CLUB.

AFTER the musical club has been organized, the leader will find that the successful club requires continual, but very enjoyable, work. The necessity for a good, steady plan is apparent to all those experienced in club work. The most feasible plans fall along the following lines:

(*a*) Historical.
(*b*) Theoretical.
(*c*) National.
(*d*) Musical forms.

The historical plan is given first importance, since it is almost impossible to appreciate thoroughly different phases of the art of music without a good fundamental knowledge of musical history. In the case of a senior class it would be an excellent plan to follow the "history year" with one devoted to the study of musical theory; that is, the foundation laws of the science of music, harmony, elementary acoustics, etc.

It is difficult to study acoustics without special physical apparatus, but a few simple experiments may be conducted by the teacher with home-made apparatus and the assistance of illustrated books on the subject. The third year might be devoted to the more advanced study of musical history, combined with an attempt to study the music of the com-

posers from the national standpoint.   A course of this kind
might be arranged thus:

First month—Folk-songs of older nations.

Second month—Italian composers.

Third month—German composers.

Fourth month—French composers.

Fifth month—Russian composers.

Sixth month—Scandinavian composers.

Seventh month—English composers.

Eighth month—American composers.

Although a whole season could be devoted to the study of
the composers of one nation, and, in fact, many musical clubs
of adults do this, the teacher of young folks will find that
variety is the spice of music, as well as of life.   The months
should be made as comprehensive as possible.   If four meetings are held each month, the German month might, for
instance, be divided thus:

First meeting—Bach and Handel.

Second meeting—Beethoven, Mozart and Haydn.

Third meeting—Gluck, Weber, Wagner and Strauss (four
great opera composers).

Fourth meeting—Mendelssohn, Schubert, Schumann and
Brahms.

This, of course, includes only the greatest masters, but
the club member has already learned of most of the lesser
ones through the medium of "The Standard History of
Music."

STUDYING MUSICAL FORM.

A year devoted to the study of the musical forms is a
profitable one.   The months might then be arranged thus:

First month—The sonata.
Second month—The symphony.
Third month—The polonaise.
Fourth month—The waltz.
Fifth month—The mazurka and the bolero.
Sixth month—The tarantelle.
Seventh month—The nocturne and the ballade.
Eighth month—The opera.
Here, again, subdivisions will provide material enough for an entire year's study.   The opera, for instance, may be divided thus:
First month—Monteverde and Handel.
Second month—Rameau, Lully and Purcell.
Third month—Gluck and Weber.
Fourth month—Rossini, Bellini and Donizetti.
Fifth month—Gounod, Bizet and Verdi.
Sixth month—Wagner.
Seventh month—Puccini, Mascagni and Leoncavallo.
Eighth month—Strauss and Debussy.

MUSICAL PROGRAMS.

It is, of course, desirable to have a musical program connected with every club meeting, but it is not possible in all cases to secure illustrations for these programs.   While, for instance, illustrations of interest from Monteverde, Lully and Purcell, etc., are obtainable, they are sometimes difficult to secure.   Operatic arrangements from Weber, Rossini, Bellini, Donizetti, Gounod, Verdi and Wagner are common, but in securing these from your music dealer you should make it very plain what grade of difficulty you require. Wagner's music, for instance, may be procured in all grades, from a children's arrangement of the *Tannhäuser March* to the great and exceedingly difficult Liszt arrangement of the Tannhäuser overture, or the *Liebestod* from "Tristan and Isolde."

How the Sound-reproducing Machine Helps.

The club leader should always recognize the danger of attempting music far too difficult for the members and defeating the purposes of the club by such impracticable means. It is, for instance, almost impossible to secure illustrations from the operatic works of Leoncavallo, Puccini, Strauss and Debussy that can be adequately given without the paraphernalia of the opera house. Here the teacher's only alternative is the use of a good sound-reproducing machine. With the help of first-class instruments and the best records the teacher has at her service the musical advantages of an opera house costing thousands of dollars to run. In fact, this is really the only way in which an adequate idea of the real musical character of the opera can be secured in towns and cities where there are no opera houses with first-class singers.

Entertainments.

In conducting the musical club for young people, games must be devised for every meeting. These games should be as varied as possible. The game played at one meeting should be of an entirely different type from that played at the last meeting. An instance of this may be shown in the following:

GAME OF MISSING LETTERS.

(*Type 1.*)

Give the missing letters of the following names of famous musicians, and name one composition by each master:

1. Johann Sebastian B___. *Bach*
2. George Frederick H___. *Handel*
3. Johannes B___. *Brahms*
4. Charles G___. *Gounod*
5. Jean Baptiste L___. *Lully*
6. Peter I. T___. *Chaikovsky*

GAME OF PICTURES.

(*Type 2.*)

The club leader here arranges around the room from twenty to thirty pictures of famous composers. The pictures are numbered, but have no names on them. Each member is then furnished with slips of paper, having as many numbers as there are pictures, and is required to guess the pictures.

A MUSICAL SPELLING MATCH: A GAME IN EAR TRAINING.

(*Type 3.*)

The leader provides each member with a slip of paper and then explains that she will first play the scale of C major upon the keyboard, and that immediately thereafter she will play some notes of this scale, the alphabetical names of which spell some word. The pupils or members, who are so placed that they cannot see the keyboard, are then asked to listen intently and try to determine which notes are sounded, and then write down the word upon the slip of paper. This makes an excellent and instructive game for bright young folks. Here are some words to try: Ace, fed, deaf, gad, bead, cabbage, dead, bad, cage.

Other similar words can be made up, but in every case the teacher should play the scale slowly, preferably naming each note, before spelling the words on the keyboard.

Another form of this same game is musical arithmetic, in which the teacher gives the notes of the scale numerical names, instead of letters. She tells the pupils or members to put down on a line the numbers of the scale she plays, and after several lines have been given she requests them to add up the lines, awarding the prize to the first member to get the correct total.

TALKS.

Although the music club is for the purpose of studying music, it is well for the teacher or leader to widen the scope of the club work occasionally by introducing talks on interesting topics. A good story for young people, on the order of "Mrs. Wiggs of the Cabbage Patch," "Tom Sawyer," "Little Men," "Under the Lilac Bush," "The Christmas Carol," "Little Lord Fauntleroy" or "The Wizard of Oz," is always welcomed with bright eyes and renewed interest.

THE CHILD'S LOVE FOR PICTURES.

The child's love for musical pictures should also be taken into consideration. Every club leader should keep a scrapbook and take advantage of the remarkable number of musical illustrations that continually appear in the general and musical magazines. It is only within the last twenty-five years, or since the introduction of the half-tone process, that such illustrations have been available for the use of the teacher. Think for a moment what an immense interest may be added to the music club work in this way. The "postcard" reflector, a form of magic lantern operated either by gas or electricity and not requiring glass slides, which may be purchased for five dollars and upward, is of great value in enlarging these pictures or postcards and projecting them upon a screen. This adds immensely to the interest in club meetings where it can be employed. Little musical pictures framed in simple manner and hung around the meeting-room of the club add greatly to its attractiveness.

Tact in Managing the Club.

The necessity for tact in club management has already been discussed. The club leader should be quick to note any feeling of dissatisfaction and ferret out the cause. It will usually be found to result from selfishness or sulkiness, and these are best overcome by both sympathy and good-hearted ridicule. Anything resembling a clique should be quickly broken up, as the life of the club depends upon the centered interest of the members.

If the way to the man's heart is through his stomach, it will likewise be found that the way to the child's loyalty is through his appetite. Many club leaders feel that it is a mistake to give refreshments at all the meetings, but at some of the principal meetings refreshments should always be served. An attempt should be made to get away from the conventional "lemonade and cake" or "ice cream and cake." Children appreciate novelties, and their parents will often judge the teacher's breeding by a little detail of this kind. Many delicious non-alcoholic fruit punches may be made with the combination of the juices of berries and grapes and the citrus fruits with sliced fruit of other descriptions.   Dainty sandwiches made in odd shapes to catch the child's eye and filled with some new and tasty filling are remembered by young folks more than the lengthy talk on "'the origin of the fugue.'"

GETTING NEW MEMBERS.

The matter of getting new members is a very important one for the life of the club.   Unless new members are admitted, there will be no way to make up for the inevitable loss of some of the old members.   One way to make membership desirable is to restrict the number of members so that there is a waiting list of those who may desire to become members of the club. Those on the waiting list should be invited to all the open meetings and to events of importance, but be made to understand that it is impossible for them to have the benefits of the club until they become full members.   In this way many will be found who, believing that it is difficult to secure admission, will try harder to become members.   This is one of the secrets of some of the most successful fraternal orders of the country.   They make it a policy never to urge anyone to join.

Children do not like to be coaxed into doing anything, but they are very anxious to join in any work in which they are convinced they have a special interest.   A public meeting at the end of the year, exhibiting the work of the club through a musical program or otherwise, and attended by the parents of the young folks, is also another desirable means of increasing the membership of the club.

THE GROWTH OF MODERN MUSIC

Four centuries of musical development, showing the comparative length of the lives of the masters, contemporary composers, and the chief events in musical and general history.

1500	1520	1540	1560	1580	1600	1620	1640

	1515	TALLIS		1585 (*ENGLAND*)			
	1525	PALESTRINA		1594	*(ITALY)*		
	1532	LASSUS		1594	*(GERMANY)*		
			1567	MONTEVERDE			1643
				1583	FRESCOBALDI		1644
							1633

OVER

IMPORTANT EVENTS IN MUSICAL HISTORY

Invention of Music Type in 1502.	Rise of the Venetian School under A.Willaert. The Virginal first used. Josquin de Pres died 1521.	Development of the Polyphonic style by Palestrina and Lassus. Famous hymn "Old Hundred" said to have been written 1551.	The rise of the Oratorio in Italy. Rise of the Cremona School of Violinmakers. Palestrina wrote Missa Papae Marcelli 1569.	The rise of the Opera in Italy. The first Ballet produced in France.	The first Italian opera Euridice by Peri performed 1600. The first real oratorio, "The Representation of the Soul and the Body" by Cavaliere performed 1600.	The first German opera "Daphne" produced 1627. Monteverde makes notable reforms in harmony.	

CONTEMPORARY EVENTS IN GENERAL HISTORY

First colonization of America in 1513. Balboa discovered the Pacific Ocean 1514. Tintoretto, famous Italian artist born 1512.	Diet of Worms 1521 Protestant Reformation. Jesuit society founded 1534. Rafael, Italian painter died 1520. Erasmus, educator died 1536.	Religious wars in Germany. Spencer, English poet born 1552. Cevantes, Spanish author born 1547.	Destruction of the Spanish Armada by England. Galilei, Italian scientist born 1564. Shakespeare, English dramatist born 1564. Rubens, Dutch artist born 1577.	Edict of Nantes, guaranteeing religious toleration in France 1598. Cromwell, English reformer born 1599. Mary,Queen of Scots beheaded 1587.	The Netherlands arose to power and importance. Rembrandt, Dutch painter born 1607. Thirty Years War commenced 1618-1648.	Puritan pilgrims land in America 1620. Dryden, English poet born 1632. Molière, French dramatist born 1622.	

1640	1660	1680	1700	1720	1740	1760	178

1643 (ITALY)
1644 (ITALY)
1633　LULLY　1687 (ITALY)
1653　CORELLI　1713
1658　PURCELL　1695 (ENGLAND)
1659　A. SCARLATTI　1725 (ITALY)
1668　COUPERIN　1733 (FRANCE)
1683　D. SCARLATTI　1757 (ITALY)
1683　RAMEAU　1764 (FRANCE)
1685　J. S. BACH　1750 (GERMANY)
1685　HANDEL　1759 (GERMANY)
1692　TARTINI　1770 (ITALY)
1714　K. P. E. BACH
1714　GLUCK
1728　PICCINI
1732　HAYDN
1734　SACCHINI
1741　GRÉTRY
1752　CLEMENTI
1756　MOZART
1760　CHERUB
1761　DUSS
1763　MÉ
1770
1774
1775
177

IMPORTANT EVENTS IN MUSICAL HISTORY

The rise of the French Opera under Lully. First opera house opened in Venice, (1637). Rise of the French opera.	A. Scarlatti introduced many epoch making innovations in opera and in oratorio. Couperin writes first instruction book for Clavier.	A. Scarlatti introduced the "Aria". Corelli developed the Sonata. Professorship of Music founded at Cambridge 1684.	The Pianoforte invented by B. Cristofori in 1710-1711. Handel's first English oratorio "Esther" produced in 1720.	Bach's "Passion" produced in 1729. Rameau published the first important book on Harmony.	Handel's "Messiah" produced in Dublin, Ireland 1741. C. P. E. Bach invented new fingering for the clavichord.	Gluck's opera "Orfeo" produced in 1764. War of the Gluckists and Piccinists in Paris in 1776.

CONTEMPORARY EVENTS IN GENERAL HISTORY

Reign of Louis XIV in France. Oliver Cromwell protector of England.	Dean Swift English author born 1667. Addison, English author born 1672. Milton, English poet died 1674.	King William's War. Alexander Pope, English poet born 1688. Voltaire, famous French author born.	Peter the Great rules in Russia. Dr. Samuel Johnson, English author born 1709. B. Franklin American Statesman and Scientist born 1706.	Oliver Goldsmith, English author born 1728. George Washington American statesman and soldier born 1732. Frederick the Great became King of Prussia 1740.	French and Indian War in America 1756-1763. Lord Nelson English sailor born 1758. Goethe, German poet born 1749.	American Revolution 1775-1783. Heinrich Heine, German poet born 1797. Scott, English poet born 1771.

THE GROWTH OF MODERN MUSIC
(Concluded)

1780	1800	1820	1840	1860	1880	1900	1910

IMPORTANT EVENTS IN MUSICAL HISTORY

							Strauss' Salome produced 1905.
Mozart's Don Giovanni produced 1781. Haydn's Creation produced 1798	Beethoven's opera Fidelio produced 1805. Upright Piano introduced.	Weber's opera Der Freischütz produced 1821. Mendelssohn's oratorio St. Paul produced 1836.	Mendelssohn's Elijah produced 1846. Leipsic Conservatory established 1843.	Wagner's Music Dramas Tristan and Isolde, Die Meistersinger, and Der Nibelungen Ring produced.	Wagner's Parsifal produced 1882. Verdi's Falstaff produced 1893.		Debussy's Pelléas et Mélisande produced 1906.

CONTEMPORARY EVENTS IN GENERAL HISTORY

| Division of Poland 1793. French Revolution 1789. Byron English poet born 1788. | War of 1812 in America. Napoleon ruled in France. Dickens born 1812. | Monroe doctrine established in America, 1823. | Mexican War, 1845. T. Edison born 1847. First Trans-Atlantic submarine cable laid 1858. | Civil War in the United States 1861. Phonograph invented by T. Edison 1877. Franco-Prussian War 1870-71. | Spanish-American War 1898. Roentgen Rays (X Rays) discovered in 1896. | | Russian-Japanese War 1904. Invention of the Aeroplane. |

1788 (GERMANY)
1787 (GERMANY)

PICCINI 1800 (ITALY)
HAYDN 1809 (AUSTRIA)
1786 (ITALY)
GRÉTRY 1813 (FRANCE)
CLEMENTI 1832 (ITALY)
MOZART 1791 (AUSTRIA)
CHERUBINI 1842 (ITALY)
DUSSEK 1812 (BOHEMIA)
MÉHUL 1817 (FRANCE)
1770 BEETHOVEN 1827 (GERMANY)
1774 SPONTINI 1851 (ITALY)
1775 BOIELDIEU 1834 (FRANCE)
1778 HUMMEL 1837 (GERMANY)
1784 SPOHR 1859 (GERMANY)
1786 VON WEBER 1826 (GERMANY)
1791 MEYERBEER 1864 (GERMANY)
1791 CZERNY 1857 (AUSTRIA)
1792 ROSSINI 1868 (ITALY)
1797 SCHUBERT 1828 (AUSTRIA)
1801 BELLINI 1835 (ITALY)
1803 BERLIOZ 1869 (FRANCE)
1809 MENDELSSOHN 1847 (GERMANY)
1810 SCHUMANN 1856 (GERMANY)
1810 CHOPIN 1849 (POLAND)
1811 LISZT 1886 (HUNGARY)
1813 WAGNER 1883 (GERMANY)
1813 VERDI 1901 (ITALY)
1818 GOUNOD 1893 (FRANCE)
1829 RUBINSTEIN 1894 (RUSSIA)
1833 BRAHMS 1897 (GERMANY)
1835 SAINT-SAËNS (FRANCE)
1840 TSCHAIKOWSKY 1893 (RUSSIA)
1843 GRIEG 1907 (NORWAY)
1854 MOSZKOWSKI (GERMANY)
1857 ELGAR (ENGLAND)
1858 PUCCINI (ITALY)
1861 MAC DOWELL 1908 (AMERICA)
1861 CHAMINADE (FRANCE)
1862 DEBUSSY (FRANCE)
1864 R STRAUSS (GERMANY)
1869 WOLF (GERMANY)
1873 REGER (GERMANY)

INDEX TO MAP OF MUSICAL EUROPE.

To find the birthplace of any composer given on the map of musical Europe: First locate the perpendicular column indicated by the letter of the alphabet; follow this column down until the horizontal section indicated by the numeral is found. The name of the composer and the city will be found in the square where the two columns intersect.

INDEX